Property Taxes, Housing and the Cities

Property Taxes, Housing and the Cities

George E. Peterson
Urban Institute

Arthur P. Solomon
Massachusetts Institute
of Technology

Hadi Madjid
Arthur D. Little, Inc.

William C. Apgar, Jr.
National Bureau of
Economic Research

Lexington Books
D.C. Heath and Company
Lexington, Massachusetts
Toronto   London

Library of Congress Cataloging in Publication Data

Main entry under title:

Property tax and urban blight.

    1. Property tax—United States. 2. Cities and towns—United States.
I. Peterson, George E.
HJ4120.P673   336.2'2'0973   73-11673
ISBN 0-669-91025-2

Published simultaneously in Canada.

Printed in the United States of America.

International Standard Book Number: 0-669-91025-2

Library of Congress Catalog Card Number: 73-11673

Contents

List of Tables

Figure

Foreword

During the decade of the 1960s, the United States faced a formidable challenge to the responsiveness of its institutions of government. At stake was the credibility of government—at all levels—which had failed to respond to the needs of the nation's poor and disenfranchised.

Today the challenge of the 1960s is still with us. But it has been compounded by a new and different kind of challenge to the credibility of government. Ten years ago, we were dealing with a relatively identifiable target. Today, we face a vague feeling of frustration and cynicism—not that government *will* not respond, but that it *can* not.

This erosion of confidence in government is rooted in the most basic issues with which government must be concerned. To those who feel frustrated, there are many symbols of the remoteness and inflexibility of government. The property tax is one such symbol.

For many decades, the local property tax has been the subject of extensive debate and criticism. By and large, discussion of the tax in the past centered on basic questions such as the merits and usage of the tax, as it was evolving in this country, versus those of other revenue-raising methods.

Within the past ten years, however, the focus of the debate has shifted. As the property tax bite has grown, the general public has become increasingly conscious of the arbitrariness and inefficiency of the tax, and has joined in the call for its reform. Today, public concern over inequities in the property tax structure is at its highest level in many years, and grows more bitter with every day that appeals for reform go unheeded.

The causes for this frustration and discontent have been well documented. For too long, the average property taxpayer in most states has been at the mercy of inexpert local officials, arbitrary bureaucracies, and privileged interests. Antiquated administrative practices and insufficient commitment of resources have prevented even responsible officials from protecting the public interest.

Above and beyond such basic concerns as these, the inequities of the property tax have been highlighted in relation to a number of important areas of public policy. One such area is the use of property tax revenues as a principal source for financing local public education.

In March of this year, the Supreme Court of the United States added its voice to the call for property tax reform. Although the majority opinion of the Court was that it could not decree reforms in present property tax administration practices which result in discrimination in school financing, the Court nevertheless issued a strong appeal for the states themselves to undertake badly needed reforms.

Another area of public policy in which the property tax has come to be regarded as a potentially important factor is that of land use planning, particularly in urban communities. As awareness of the crisis of our cities has spread, the relationship of the property tax to this problem has generated many theories. At one time or another, the property tax has variously been cited as a cause of urban blight, an obstacle to urban redevelopment, and a possible lever

xiii

to be used in the rebuilding of decaying urban centers. Unfortunately, the facts to support these various arguments have, until now, been inconclusive.

It is to this debate—over the role of the property tax in the urban crisis—that the following study makes an important contribution.

Commissioned by the Department of Housing and Urban Development, and conducted by Arthur D. Little Inc., this study is an analysis of the effect of property taxation policies on urban blight in 10 American cities: Atlanta, Baltimore, Chicago, Detroit, Nashville, Oklahoma City, Philadelphia, Portland (Oregon), Providence, and San Francisco. Its conclusions offer yet another indictment of the property tax as presently administered in many parts of the country.

Among the conclusions of the study are that poor property tax administration (1) is a contributing factor in urban blight; (2) is an obstacle to the upgrading of poor-quality housing; and (3) discourages minority ownership of urban property. In addition, the study concludes that property tax appeal structures in many of the cities studied do not offer any real remedy to the average taxpayer for inadequate assessment practices.

In more specific terms, the study reveals that in five of the ten cities studied, the median effective tax rate in blighted neighborhoods is many times higher than that in stable or upward transitional neighborhoods. In most cases, according to the analysis, such inequities are principally a result of confused reassessment policies which often bear no relation to actual market values and trends.

Finally, in a detailed examination of the property tax structures in the ten cities, the report provides an important case study in how outmoded property tax systems can contribute directly to severe tax inequities, and, indirectly, to urban decay.

In 1963, the states received thoroughgoing, professional recommendations for assessment reform from the Advisory Commission on Intergovernmental Relations. Since that time, the case for reform has grown continually stronger.

Yet, in spite of the overwhelming body of evidence of the need for reform, the response of government has been almost universally disappointing. The property tax remains the most inefficiently and arbitrarily administered of all taxes, even while it continues to constitute the single largest source of tax revenue for local units of government throughout the nation.

The future of the property tax itself is not really in doubt. Few would argue for its total abandonment, at least not at any time in the near future.

What is in doubt is when—or even if—government will respond with a commitment to make this form of taxation fair and workable. The report which follows will hopefully bring such a response closer to reality. If so, this will indeed be a worthy accomplishment.

Edmund S. Muskie
U.S. Senator

Acknowledgements

How property taxes affect housing investment and maintenance has been the subject of much speculation. But until the study on which this book is based was done, there has been little empirical data that indicates how property owners' decisions about rehabilitation and maintenance are actually affected by the impost.

Thus, the authors acknowledge a very large debt of thanks to the 228 property owners who agreed to participate in the study. They opened their books to the study team, and spent many hours responding to questions, describing their investment strategies, explaining their problems, and giving insight into the complex of forces, including the property tax, that bear upon their operations. The study's statistical limitations are more than offset, we feel, by the richness of interpretation they gave us through dialog.

We also wish to thank the assessors and their staffs in the 10 cities we studied. Their aid was invaluable in helping us to locate property owners to interview. They patiently explained their assessment formulae, and gave us access to records showing property locations and tax rates.

We cannot fail to mention the role of the Economic Analysis section within the U.S. Department of Housing and Urban Development. Under the direction of Arnold Diamond, HUD conceived the need for such a study and awarded the contract for it to Arthur D. Little, Inc., the Cambridge, Mass., research and consulting firm. HUD, through Diamond and his colleagues, maintained a strong critical interest throughout, from the design of questionnaires to the tabulation of results. This book draws heavily on the ADL report to HUD. Neither the ADL report nor this book, of course, necessarily represent the views of the Federal Government. The authors must bear full responsibility for the interpretations and conclusions drawn from the study.

The study and the book would not have been possible without the legwork and headwork assistance provided by Arthur D. Little staff and consultants. For the design of questionnaires, we are indebted to Prof. Raymond C. Bauer of the Harvard Business School and to Dr. Anton S. Morton and Ellen I. Metcalf of ADL. Field work in the ten cities and valuable professional support were contributed by Alan H. Balfour, Fred L. Bell, John C. Bruckman, Alan D. Donheiser, Robert Dubinsky, Harry G. Foden, Susan K. Moulton, John Pitkin, Ruth Prokoff, Linda A. Sallop, Janet T. Shanklin, and Ann H. Zubko. Dr. Hadi Madjid served as project director for ADL.

George E. Peterson
Arthur P. Solomon
William C. Apgar, Jr.
Hadi Madjid

1 Introduction

Economics today rides the crest of intellectual respectability and popular acclaim . . . second only to that which was given to physicists and space experts a few years ago. But I submit that the consistently indifferent performance in practical applications is in fact a symptom of a fundamental imbalance in the present state of our discipline. The weak and all too slowly growing empirical foundation clearly cannot support the proliferating superstructure of pure, or should I say, speculative economic theory. Alongside the mounting pile of elaborate theoretical models we see a fast-growing stock of equally intricate statistical tools. These are intended to stretch to the limit the meager supply of available facts.

Wassily Leontief,
Presidential Address
American Economic Association,
December 29, 1970

Few social institutions boast a better record for surviving public criticism than the local property tax. For decades the property tax has been attacked by prominent experts as a tax whose "defects . . . it would appear, are beyond remedy,"[1] as "beyond doubt one of the worst taxes known in the civilized world,"[2] and as an "inferior tax [which] becomes a monstrous one if applied at high enough rates."[3] Despite this barrage of professional criticism, however, property taxation continues to account for the bulk of locally raised public revenue in the United States, just as it has throughout the country's history. In 1973 total property tax receipts came to some $45 billion. And the locally raised portion represented about 85 percent of all tax revenue collected at the municipal level. While it is true that since World War II the property tax has slipped into third place on the list of tax-raising devices in the United States, falling behind the federally administered personal income and social security taxes, for many years the share of property taxes in national income accounts has risen gradually now standing at somewhat more than 4 percent.

The criticisms lodged against the property tax may be conveniently summarized under three headings. First, the property tax is alleged to be a regressive tax,

1

in the sense that it seems to place a disproportionate financial burden on the poor, especially as compared to alternative means of taxation such as the income tax. In the most common version of this argument, the property tax is compared to a sales tax which instead of being levied on luxury goods, like jewelry or restaurant meals, is imposed on perhaps the most vital of man's necessities: his home. This criticism is aimed at the choice of property, especially residential property, as the tax base.

Second, the property tax is alleged to have inequitable effects across jurisdictions, since wealthy communities are able to raise a given amount of public revenue per household at lower tax *rates* than are poor communities. A criticism to this effect forms the basis of recent court decisions which have held that the use of local property taxation to finance public schooling violates the equal service provision requirements of some state constitutions. In this instance, the objection is not so much to the choice of property as the tax base, since a tax on local incomes (say) would create similar disparities between wealthy and poor districts. Rather, it is the local character of the property-tax system that is judged to be inequitable. Critics argue that expenditures for basic public services like schooling should not be dependent upon local ability to pay for them.

Finally, the property tax commonly is thought to disrupt the operation of the housing market. As economists long have pointed out, placing a tax on a good must either raise the price consumers pay for the good or lower the profit producers can earn from supplying it. In either case, the imposition of a tax is likely to lead to a lower level of provision of the good in question. The housing market is thought to be no exception. If this reasoning is right, an increase in property-tax rates may lead directly to a lower supply of new housing, or (what is likely to be more readily observable) it may discourage upgrading and rehabilitation of the current housing stock and accelerate the decision of landlords in low-income areas to abandon their housing altogether. Variations in the effective rate of property taxation from one neighborhood or community to the next should likewise affect the housing market, since a comparison of tax burdens is one of the calculations that a prudent household will make before deciding where to live.

While the present study sheds light on each of the above areas of concern, its principal goal is to clarify the effects that the property tax has on the operation of the urban housing market—especially the rental sector of that market. This is one of those fields where, as Wassily Leontief has pointed out, theoretical speculation has far outrun factual understanding. Economists have tried to compensate for the "meager supply of facts" about how housing decisions are made by devising increasingly sophisticated statistical analyses to apply to the available body of housing data. Unfortunately, however, most of these data are mere numbers, whose adequate interpretation requires some comprehension of the market behavior that produces them.

The first aim of this study, then, is to provide the reader with a substantial set of facts about the property tax and urban-housing markets, which were collected from several months of interviews with housing investors in ten cities. At the same time, we try to interpret these facts by placing them in the context of landlords' operating decisions, and by identifying their consequences for a city's housing market as a whole. This has required us to mediate between three different types of language: the language of the real estate operators and managers whose behavior we want to describe, the language of elementary statistics, which best summarizes numerical information acquired in the course of our interviews, and the language of basic economic theory, which makes it possible to analyze the aggregate effect of individual investors' decisions.

Scope of the Study

As shown in Table 1-1, the data underlying the study were gathered in the course of interviews with property owners and local officials concerning the operation of 420 housing parcels in ten cities: Atlanta, Baltimore, Chicago, Detroit, Nashville, Oklahoma City, Philadelphia, Portland (Oregon), Providence, and San Francisco. These cities originally were selected by the Department of Housing and Urban Development as representative of the wide range of urban-housing conditions that exists in the United States. In a municipality like Oklahoma City, for example, almost 80 percent of the families live in single-family homes, while in cities like Chicago or Providence less than one-fourth of the households occupy single-family residences. In several of the sample cities (e.g., Atlanta or San Francisco), urban residential properties are in high demand in almost all neighborhoods; while in other cities (e.g., Detroit or Philadelphia), housing values have plummeted over large sections of the cities as vacancy rates and abandonment have spiraled upward.

It is not enough, however, to structure an empirical sample so as to capture the most important differences in housing-market conditions among different cities. Within every major city there exist what we may call distinctive housing submarkets. The different neighborhoods of a city tend to specialize in satisfying demand for different kinds of housing. One neighborhood may provide low-quality housing at relatively low prices; another, high-quality housing at high prices.

Table 1-1
Sample Distribution by City (All Properties)

Atlanta	46	Oklahoma City	41
Baltimore	43	Philadelphia	46
Chicago	41	Portland	42
Detroit	41	Providence	40
Nashville	40	San Francisco	40

Trends in housing prices may differ as well. It is not uncommon to find that while prices surge upward in one part of a city, elsewhere in the same city properties are being abandoned because they cannot generate an economic rent. Because the effect that property taxation has on a housing market depends so crucially on the economic conditions of that market, even a uniform property tax may have drastically different consequences for the different neighborhoods of a city. In addition, of course, there are important differences in the size of rental housing structures and the characteristics of owners that can greatly affect the interaction of the property tax and housing supply.

We have attempted to deal with this diversity of housing-market conditions by structuring our sample of properties according to three parameters. For each city we created a three-way classification by *property type, total number of units owned or managed by an investor, and neighborhood housing market conditions.* Properties were identified, first, as either single unit or multifamily rental structures, or owner-occupied single-family homes. Other studies have indicated that the owners of these property types are likely to behave differently in the real-estate market. For instance, George Sternlieb has emphasized that over half of all slum properties are owned by people who regard themselves as amateurs in the real-estate market, for whom rental income is only a supplement to a livelihood earned in other occupations.[4] Designing public policies to reach these owners may require far different measures from those that will successfully reach large-scale professional operators. Consequently, we have also divided the owners of rental housing into two size categories: those who own forty or fewer units and those who own more than forty units. Any division such as this contains an element of arbitrariness, but tests in our trial city of Providence indicated that this division represented the approximate cut-off point between investors who perceived themselves primarily as real-estate operators and investors who looked upon real estate as a sideline.

The third parameter used to stratify the sample properties was neighborhood type. As long as neighborhoods form well-defined housing submarkets, all of the factors that determine neighborhood "quality" should be reflected in the level and trend of neighborhood property values. Our procedure, therefore, was to define neighborhoods in terms of price trends. In each city, we identified four geographic areas that coincide with our four neighborhood types on the basis of the level and change in property values over the last six years.

Thus, in each city, we identified a stable neighborhood (where property values were relatively constant at a high level or increasing at the city-wide average rate), an upward transitional neighborhood (where property values were increasing at an above average rate); a downward transitional neighborhood (where property values were declining) and a blighted neighborhood (where property values were steady at a very low level or sinking toward zero).

In each city, neighborhoods that fit this classification were identified on the basis of two or three days of preliminary interviews with the local assessor and his staff, local planning agencies, and local bank officials. Once a specific neighborhood was identified as belonging to one of the submarket classifications, several owners of property in that district were contacted for interview through random processes, while other owners were selected because conversations with bank officials or neighborhood community organizations indicated that they were illustrative of important types of economic activity underway in the neighborhoods selected for study.

Altogether, complete interviews were conducted with 184 owners of rental stock and 45 homeowners, regarding the operations of 420 central-city parcels. Combining the three classifying characteristics—property type, owner size, and neighborhood type—we established a property stratification matrix of the kind presented in Tables 1-2 and 1-3. The numbers in each of the cells of Table 1-2 indicate the number of properties whose owners typically were interviewed for a single city. In addition, in each city three or four owners of commercial property were interviewed. Within the neighborhood boundaries defined for the study, the sample properties contained just over 2 percent of the total number of housing units. A reproduction of the investor interview format is included as Appendix D.

Despite the considerable effort that was made to assure that the sampled properties were representative of local housing-market activity, the statistical basis of the sample is too slender and not sufficiently random to permit accurate statistical analysis. Our hope is that the in-depth interviews with property owners will make the data more intelligible than would have been possible from purely statistical analysis on a larger data base. Forced to choose between large-scale data collection without extensive interviewing, and the accumulation

Table 1-2
Property Stratification Matrix (Typical City)

	Stable	Upward Transitional	Downward Transitional	Blighted
Homeowner	1	1	1	1
Investor				
2 to 40 units	3	3	3	3
41 or more units	6	5	5	5
Commercial	3			

Table 1-3
Property Stratification Matrix (Entire Sample)

	Stable	Upward Transitional	Downward Transitional	Blighted
Homeowner	13	11	11	10
Investor				
2 to 40 units	19	35	37	29
41 or more units	72	54	41	58
Commercial	30			

of data on fewer properties with extensive property-owner interviews to enrich our understanding of the data, we deliberately opted for the latter approach.

Outline of the Study

Following this introduction, Chapter 2 summarizes the analytical approach adopted throughout the study. This approach seeks to place information about the individual investor and his parcel in the context of a specific neighborhood-housing submarket. Our emphasis on market analysis contrasts with previous writers' almost exclusive concentration on cash-flow studies, some of the difficulties of which are pointed out in this chapter.

Chapter 3 sets forth the principal descriptive facts about the neighborhood-housing markets included in the sample. It shows that in several cities there is a systematic overassessment of properties in blighted and downward transitional neighborhoods and an underassessment of properties in stable and upward transitional neighborhoods. These neighborhood variations in assessment rates result in dramatic variations in the effective rate of property taxation paid by parcels located in different parts of the same city. In several cities the systematic assessment bias against low-income properties contributes heavily to the regressivity of the property tax. Variations in effective property-tax rates by neighborhood are shown to be much larger than intracity variations according to any other means of classification of property such as the age or size of individual structures or characteristics of the owners.

The second half of Chapter 3 examines the cities' practice as regards assessment of property improvements, in order to evaluate the contention that the property tax actively discourages adequate maintenance of the housing stock. Our data indicate that in most cities housing rehabilitation costing less than $3,000 per unit is not reassessed at all. Moreover, those parcels that are reassessed typically have their assessed valuation increased by much less than the full cost of the rehabilitation. From this evidence, it would seem that the economic literature may have exaggerated the actual disincentive effect of property taxation on the maintenance and upgrading of the housing stock. This conclusion is reinforced by the responses investors gave when asked if they viewed reassessment as an important obstacle to rehabilitation. The great majority of investors ranked fear of reassessment among the least important obstacles, significantly behind such considerations as the strength of neighborhood housing demand or the availability of financing.

Chapter 4 scrutinizes the market for low-income properties. It concludes that, while the problem of low-quality housing is attributable primarily to the low purchasing power of poor families, and thus is beyond remedy by alterations in the property tax, the administration of the property tax does contribute to the collapse of many low-income housing markets into what have been called "crisis ghettoes."

Considerable evidence is presented in this chapter to indicate that where stable low-income housing markets are functioning well, properties tend to be operated by recent purchasers. Unlike investors who acquired their properties ten or twenty years ago—and are saddled with capital losses that cripple their ability to look at a parcel in a blighted neighborhood as a fresh investment— these recent purchasers usually acquired their parcels at extremely low prices, with a full knowledge of neighborhood conditions, and with the intention of effecting selective improvements so as to capitalize on the unsatisfied demand for moderate quality housing that exists in blighted neighborhoods.

We argue that a once-for-all equalization of assessment procedures leading to equalization of effective property-tax rates might have a significant effect on the low-income housing market. By reducing the costs of operating rental properties, property tax cuts in these markets would lead to a modest increase in property values and very likely induce significant transfer of properties from older, absentee, white landlords to neighborhood owners who are more willing and capable of managing low-quality housing.

Chapter 5 investigates the condition of the downward transitional neighborhood, whose logical terminus is that of blight, unless the downward spiral of neighborhood deterioration can be arrested. The chapter centers on the role that property-tax regulations can play in accelerating or retarding this downward spiral.

In Chapter 6 we shift our focus from the private market for low- and moderate-income housing to the publicly subsidized market and examine the impact that the property tax has on subsidized housing. In our interviews numerous investors in subsidized housing cited the uncertainty of future property-tax obligations as one of the primary risks involved in the operation of subsidized housing. This risk arises from the fact that no federal guidelines exist as to how subsidized properties should be taxed. In some cities subsidized parcels are assessed at construction cost; in others, assessment is fixed at the property's estimated market value if it had to be sold on the private market without its subsidy. In still other cities subsidized projects pay a fixed percentage of rent receipts in lieu of ordinary property-tax payments. More importantly, each of these arrangements represents a mere administrative decision, which the city can reverse at any time, thereby drastically altering a parcel's property-tax liability. Given the existing rate of default on subsidized housing, it seems foolish to augment still further the risks that management must cope with by failing to give landlords some consistent guidelines on their property tax liability.

Chapter 7 discusses the upward transitional neighborhoods, where most of a city's rehabilitation investment typically is concentrated. This chapter analyzes the "externality" or neighborhood effects of housing improvements in areas undergoing vigorous upgrading. It emphasizes that property-tax policy can either encourage or discourage neighborhood revival, depending on whether assessments are adjusted to reflect neighborhood increases in property values or the increments in value to individual properties that result from property-specific improvements.

Chapter 8 deals with stable neighborhoods. It discusses the effects of tax and public-service competition between stable central-city neighborhoods and the suburbs. The chapter gives special attention to the effect that property-tax-base equalization among jurisdictions would have on metropolitan housing markets.

Chapter 9 moves from the perspective of the investor to the perspective of the assessor. In this chapter we examine the differences in assessment policies and practices that make some cities' assessment procedures more effective than others. The relative effectiveness of different cities' assessment practices is then compared with the budgetary costs of assessment to gain some indication of the cost-effectiveness of different assessment techniques.

Chapter 10 reports investors' and assessors' evaluations of various proposals for replacing the present property tax. Rather surprisingly, we found little dissatisfaction with the principle of property-value taxation, nor much enthusiasm for proposed modifications of the present tax system. In particular, investors and assessors alike were strongly opposed to either land taxation or the use of differential tax rates for land and structures.

Chapter 11 concludes the book with a brief discussion of the major policy recommendations that follow from our analysis. Emphasis is placed on the reforms necessary to make the property-tax system more equitable and effective.

A Word on the Quality of the Data

The statistical portion of this, or any other housing-market study, is no better than the quality of the data upon which it is based. For this reason we owe it to the reader to make explicit those reservations about the data he would want to keep in mind if he had collected the data himself. Early in this study we ran into an unexpected dilemma. Our interview design requested a considerable amount of specific financial information from each investor. The investors interviewed also were intended to be representative of those who managed properties in each neighborhood. It proved relatively easy to interview representative investors in the sample neighborhoods. It also proved relatively easy to find investors who maintained complete financial records on their properties. However, it was impossible to meet both of these objectives simultaneously. This was not a consequence of bad will on the part of owners, although from time to time we encountered investors who were unwilling to disclose the financial details of their operation. Rather, the majority of the small owners whom we contacted simply did not maintain accurate records of their expenditures or rental receipts. We soon found that if we eliminated from our sample all those investors whose records were only partially complete and replaced them with other investors who could provide all the desired financial data, we would end up with a biased sample, in which knowledgeable or professional investors were seriously over-represented since these investors were most likely to possess adequate financial data.

In almost all cases we were able to reconstruct from recent bills and check stubs a reliable account of the investor's financial statement for the most recent year. However, for many investors it was impossible to obtain earlier records. Thus the reader will find that responses to some of the more detailed financial questions are incomplete, reflecting the inability of some respondents to provide full financial information. We have preferred to accept this partial availability of certain financial data to the alternative of structuring the sample so as to exclude amateur investors.

2

The Property Tax and Neighborhood Analysis

Most empirical studies of landlords' operation of urban rental properties have concentrated on the investor's income and expense statement as the key to understanding his maintenance decisions. It has been hypothesized, for instance, that it is crucial to discover whether properties currently are operating with a negative or near-zero cash flow or are generating a positive cash flow. The former properties are thought to be much more likely candidates for deterioration or even abandonment. While the rationale for this emphasis on cash flow rarely is made explicit, it is implied that investors look at the proceeds from their rental operation much the way a small company might look at its cash flow. If business is going well and there is money left over, some of it will be used for expansion, in this case by upgrading the income-generating property. If business is going poorly and there is a drain on funds, some cutback on capital replacement may take place in order to conserve cash. Changes in the property tax then would be important insofar as they altered the cost side of a particular investor's operating statement.

We shall present evidence in Chapters 4 and 5 that the investment behavior of many small investors conforms fairly well to this simple model. Since these investors find it difficult to borrow funds for repairs or upgrading, they often are constrained in their investment decisions by the cash flow a property generates.

The cash-flow approach to housing analysis, however, suffers from two major drawbacks. First, it often fails to distinguish among the different reasons for a change in cash flow. A cash-flow statement is the result of a wide range of supply and demand factors. Differences in the income or expense statement of a property over time or differences between two properties for a single year may reflect widely different underlying causes: dissimilar neighborhood demand for housing, fortuitous factors such as whether an owner has paid off his mortgage or not, or important differences in the ability of owners to supply the sort of housing that consumers are willing to pay for. To concentrate on the net cash flow alone is to confound these separate factors by implicitly weighting each according to the dollar change it effects in the investor's cash-flow statement without ever exploring the connection that exists between the operating statement and housing-market dynamics. Without these explicit linkages, few conclusions can be drawn from cash-flow analysis.

Secondly, the cash-flow approach treats a parcel and its operator as if they were forever conjoined. This is clearly unrealistic. To the extent that the cost elements in a cash-flow statement reflect either the current operator's efficiency

11

or the purchase price of the property, it should be obvious that these costs can change drastically if management changes or the property is transferred to a new owner. In blighted neighborhoods, for instance, it is common for properties purchased ten to fifteen years ago to produce a negative cash flow, largely because the owner is saddled with debt payments based on a purchase price exceeding the current value of the structure. If the property were to be sold today, the debt payments on the new purchase price would be so much lower that often the new purchaser could generate a positive cash flow even if he operated the parcel in the same manner. For all structures except those that should be abandoned, there is some asset price at which the property will produce a positive cash flow over the expected life of the building. If the real-estate market is functioning well, the market price of properties will adjust until each parcel would generate a positive cash flow *if* annual debt payments were made on its current value. In a perfect market, in fact, the cash flow of a parcel at any given moment would have almost no significance. The asset prices of all properties would have adjusted so that, if efficiently operated, all parcels would yield the same risk-adjusted rate of return on their current market value. Differences in cash flow then would reflect only historical accidents such as the original purchase price paid by an owner or any abnormal inefficiencies in the current operation of the property. They would provide no information whatsoever on the best, or most likely, investment strategy for a property.

This is not to deny that in practice the real-estate market is far from perfect and that elements other than dispassionate economic calculation enter into investors' decisions on whether to upgrade a property, let it run down, or perhaps abandon it altogether. A history of financial reversal, for instance, may completely alter an owner's style of management, even though in strictly economic terms the owner should regard past losses as irrelevant to present profit-maximizing decisions.[1] Recognizing these difficulties, our approach will be to look to a cash-flow statement only for clues as to the present owner's ability to manage his parcel or clues as to the financial constraints an owner is operating under. We will not argue that the size or sign of the cash flow by itself implies anything at all about the level at which a property can best be operated. In our interviewing, we found as many examples where a negative cash flow was turned around by substantially upgrading a property as we did examples where the optimal response to a negative cash flow proved to be a run-down strategy culminating in abandonment. A cash-flow statement by itself can never indicate the optimal investment strategy for a property. At most, it may signal the presence of a constraint, such as the unavailability of funds, which forecloses options for an investor, leaving him with but one choice as to how he can operate a parcel.

Confusion as to how to interpret financial statements extends throughout the literature on housing operations. In attempting to identify the causes of abandonment, for example, Akahoshi and Gass examined the cash-flow statements of abandoned buildings or buildings in danger of being abandoned. The fastest growing cost items were taken to be the precipitating causes of abandonment. In the case of Chicago, the authors observed that "maintenance, tax, and insurance costs are the key operating costs and that incomes, severely affected by non-payments, vacancies, and non-collection, are not adequate to compensate for these high costs."[2]

Upon reflection it seems clear that the scenario summarized in this cash-flow statement could be produced by a variety of circumstances, which make even the distinction between "costs" and "income" hard to maintain. It could be, as Akahoshi and Gass seem to suggest, that rising cost items lead to a cost squeeze and so to abandonment. Consider, however, an alternative explanation. The rent levels of neighborhood properties may decline in response to a declining demand for neighborhood housing. In attempting to respond to this declining demand, a landlord may try to preserve his income by renting to larger families than before or by renting to households that impose higher maintenance costs on his property. The increased usage of his building which this implies, however, may force him to make greater maintenance expenditures or effect further cutbacks in the quality of accommodations. This reduced quality may oblige him to rent to even less desirable tenants, who impose even greater maintenance expenses, until finally the owner abandons his property. In this case a decline in demand would be the true "cause" leading to abandonment, but this falloff in demand might show up as much in the form of increased maintenance expenditures as in reduced rental income.

An equally common mistake is to confuse the cash-flow situation of the particular owner of a property with the parcel's potential for generating cash flow for some future owner. George Sternlieb and Robert Burchell report the situation confronting one landlord in Newark.[3] The relevant cash-flow information is summarized in Table 2-1. Having purchased the property for $15,000, this owner was paying amortization, interest, and property taxes at a level which bore no relationship to the current value of the property. Indeed, Sternlieb and Burchell estimate the property to be worth only $6,000. They conclude: "with income/expense indices such as these, it is inconceivable that this cash flow picture could continue." They proceed to discuss the likelihood of demolition or other end-game strategies.

However, the negative cash flow of the parcel shown in Table 2-1 is not a characteristic of the property at all. An astute owner should be successful in reducing the property's assessed valuation to its current market value and so halving the property-tax liability which the property carries. Furthermore, if the property changed hands at the true, reduced value, a sharp reduction in interest and amortization payments would result, even if the terms of a new mortgage were somewhat less favorable than the present one. In short, what appears to be a hopeless situation could be vastly improved simply by revising amortization, interest, and property tax payments to reflect current reality, rather than

Table 2-1
Cash Flow of a Typical Residential Property (Newark, N.J.–Spring 1972)

Income	
2 Apts. @ $140/Mo =	$3,360/Yr
(Assuming no vacancy)	
Expenses	
Amortization/interest	$ 930
(6%, 30 yrs $13,500)	
Maintenance	200
Heating	400
Insurance (risk pool)	300
Electricity	290
Water	40
	$2,160/Yr
Cash Flow (before taxes)	+$1,200
Annual property tax	1,200
Net cash flow	0

2½ story frame dwelling, 2-family nonresident owner, parcel assessed value $15,000, market value $6,000, annual property tax $1,200. Estimated demolition costs $1,900.

Source: George Sternlieb and Robert Burchell, *Residential Abandonment: The Tenement Landlord Revisited*, op. cit., p. 371.

historical accident. Such a revision would be likely to occur if the property were sold.

In general, a structure's operating income will convey a better indication of its profitability than its cash flow. Operating income is the total that remains from gross rents after subtraction of expenditures on maintenance and operations. It is this amount which is capitalized into the asset value of a property. However, even the operating income of a building may turn out to be highly variable depending upon the skill of the person who operates it. Our interviews identified a considerable number of investors who purchased properties and immediately appealed their assessment, using the lower purchase price as evidence that a building previously had been overassessed. If the appeal was successful, one important component of operating costs, property-tax liability, was reduced at once. Other new purchasers found that replacement of a heating plant or other item could significantly slash a parcel's operating expenses, or that cosmetic rehabilitation of a structure's interior could greatly augment rents. Often upon transfer of ownership, a property's financial setup changed drastically. Table 2-2 illustrates one of the most dramatic cases of turnaround. This investor in 1966 purchased a property in a quasi-blighted neighborhood. The investor at once successfully appealed the assessment, changed insurance coverage to a new company at a greatly reduced rate, repainted the interior of the building, and filled vacancies. As can be seen, by 1968 the property's operating statement bore little resemblance to that of 1966, rental income was up 50

Table 2-2
Change in Cash-Flow Statement

	1966		1968	
Gross Rent	6042		9217	
Administration		900		900
Insurance		752		327
Utilities		171		142
Maintenance and repairs		1,977		2,765
Property taxes		2,063		1,336
Operating income	179		3747	
Debt service		1,303		1,303
Cash flow	−1124		2444	

Note: This cash-flow statement of a particular investor was selected as representative of the point discussed in the text.

percent while operating costs were down, even though outlays on maintenance and repairs had increased markedly. To focus on this property's net cash flow in 1966, or even the magnitude of individual cost items, would have revealed nothing about the quality level at which the parcel could most efficiently be operated.

The Property Tax and the Supply of Housing

Throughout this book we will make references to the fact that an increase in property-tax rates may be shifted forward to the tenant in the form of higher rents, or may be absorbed by the landlord in the form of lower profits, depending upon market conditions.[4] Most likely of all, some of the increased tax burden will fall on both parties. It may refresh the reader's recollection if we sketch the effect of a property-tax increase in terms of the traditional demand-supply diagram shown in Figure 2-1. The line SS in the diagram represents the original supply curve of housing and the line DD the demand for housing. Imposition of a uniform property tax can be represented as a shift upwards in the supply curve, SS. After a tax increase, at every level of housing supply the owner must cover all his previous costs plus the additional tax payments. With typically shaped curves such as those shown in the diagram, this shift upwards in the cost of supplying rental units will both raise the price of housing and lower the quantity of housing that is provided. Increases in the price of housing are easily observed as rent increases. Decreases in the quantity of housing may be harder to observe. The "quantity" of housing stock is a composite measure of the number of dwelling units and their quality. A diminution of the housing stock can take the form of a reduction in the number of dwelling units or a reduction in average "quality," that is to say, standard of maintenance and services provided by units. Imposition of a residential property tax usually is thought to have both effects. It discourages some investment in rehabilitation and maintenance and at the same time retards new construction. Reducing property-tax rates would have a reverse effect: in general, it would both lower housing prices and stimulate more housing investment.

Figure 2-1 illustrates the shift to a new equilibrium caused by imposing a property tax. After imposition of the tax (t), the price of housing (P_2) is higher and the quantity of housing (Q_2) is lower than before the tax. Whether property

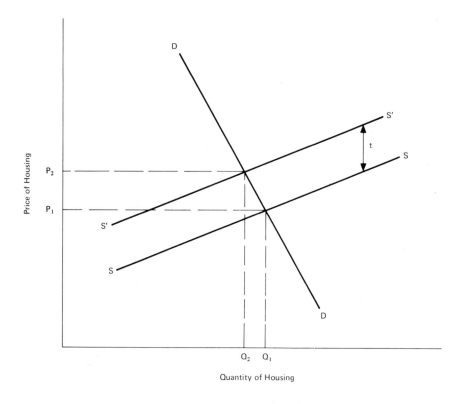

Note: DD is the demand curve for housing

SS is the supply curve for housing prior to introduction of property tax

S'S' is the supply curve for housing after the imposition of tax t.

Figure 2-1. Shift in Equilibrium with an Increase in Property Taxes

taxes have their principal effect on the quality of housing or on rent levels depends on the elasticity of the supply and demand curves—that is, the responsiveness of housing supply and demand to price changes.

The more elastic is the supply of housing—that is, the flatter is the supply curve, SS, in Figure 2-1—the greater will be the price adjustment that accompanies a tax increase. While it could be argued that reducing the property-tax burden will benefit tenants only if substantial improvement of the housing stock results, this view disregards consumer preferences. For poor families, there are many necessities to be purchased. Better housing, desirable as it is, may seem less urgent to a family than other needs. If the savings from a property-tax reduction are passed on to the tenant, he will have the choice of obtaining improved housing for the same rent as before or spending the money saved from lower rents on other commodities. However, if the objective of governmental policy is to improve the welfare of tenants, it does not matter greatly which choice families make. Housing or tax policy could benefit tenants substantially while having little discernible effect on housing conditions.

The crucial question is whether a reduction in the property-tax rate will be passed on to the tenant at all. If landlords were able to maintain the same rents, in the face of reduced property taxes, the entire effect of a tax reduction would be to make landlords richer rather than help tenants. Who ultimately benefits from a tax reduction, or any other reduction in the cost of supplying housing, depends on the competitiveness of the housing market. If the owners of housing must compete with one another to attract tenants, either by price cutting or undertaking minor repairs, then eventually the cost reductions achieved by a tax cut will be passed on to the tenant. If the housing market is more oligopolistically organized, so that owners can fix prices, free from competition, the principal beneficiaries of tax reduction may well be the landlords. The degree of competition among suppliers of housing thus is crucial in determining the welfare implications of property-tax policy. The neighborhood chapters of this study indicate that housing investors behave more competitively than generally is conceded. If this is so, a substantial part of the benefits of any property-tax reduction would be passed on to tenants, either in the form of improved housing conditions at the same rent, or in the form of lower rents.

3

Variation in Property-Tax Rates

This chapter summarizes the basic data on property-tax rates which were collected in our investigation. It establishes the range of variation in tax levels by neighborhood and city, and examines the incremental rates at which cities tax improvements to the housing stock.

The sample cities fall into two groups. In one (Baltimore, Chicago, Philadelphia, and Providence), a clear neighborhood pattern emerges in which poor-quality housing, occupied by low-income tenants, pays property taxes at a substantially higher rate than property in wealthy neighborhoods. Since legislation applicable to each of the cities calls for uniform rates of taxation for all residential real estate, neighborhood rate differentials like these place a tax burden on low-quality housing which, by the standard of existing legislation, is inequitable. In contrast to these older cities, no systematic neighborhood variation in tax rates was discernible in Atlanta, Detroit, Nashville, Oklahoma City, Portland, or San Francisco.

The sample evidence compiled on incremental tax rates was surprising. In most cities, moderate improvements to the housing stock were not assessed at all, while major improvements were assessed at substantially less than cost. As a result, the average incremental rate of taxation on improvements was extremely low. This evidence indicates that the marginal disincentive which the property tax provides to housing investment may be less than generally thought.[1]

City Differentials in Property-Tax Rates

The cities in our sample differed substantially both in their rates of property taxation and in the degree of their reliance on the property tax to raise revenue. Table 3-1 presents a city-by-city breakdown of property-tax receipts as a proportion of all local revenue. Table 3-2 displays the 1970 property tax rate in each city. The first column of Table 3-2 presents the "legal" effective tax rate for 1970, assuming that assessment/sales ratios within each city met the legislatively mandated target level. The second column gives the "actual" median effective tax rate. This "actual" tax rate is based on the true median assessment/sales ratio for each city as of 1966 rather than the target ratio. In a well-functioning assessment system, the values for columns 1 and 2 would be approximately equal. Data on actual assessment/sales ratios are collected by the Census of Governments and are not yet available subsequent to 1966.

19

Table 3-1
Per Capita Expenditures and Revenue by City (1966)

City	Per Capita Expenditures	Per Capita Total Locally Raised Revenue	Per Capita Local Property Tax Revenues	Residential Property Assessments as a % of all Locally Assessed Taxable Property
Atlanta (Fulton Co.)	$329.68	$269.96	$133.66	69.1%
Baltimore	407.29	200.49	149.36	66.0
Chicago (Cook Co.)	355.24	279.39	162.49	62.4
Detroit (Wayne Co.)	422.13	282.76	154.62	57.7
Nashville (Davidson Co.)	421.30	263.04	93.48	63.7
Oklahoma City (Oklahoma Co.)	281.74	211.84	109.69	78.9
Philadelphia	329.27	235.00	99.14	63.3
Portland (Multnomah Co.)	363.29	281.39	179.31	68.4
Providence	237.37	179.35	142.50	52.5
San Francisco	877.15	552.32	302.32	54.2

Notes: For those cities where education expenditures are assumed by the county or special school district, the county figures have been used. Expenditures includes all money paid out—net of recoveries and other correcting transactions—other than for retirement of debt, investment in securities, extension of credit, or as agency transactions. Expenditures include only external transactions of a government and exclude noncash transactions such as provision of prerequisites or other payments in kind. Population figures used for per capita calculations are for 1960.

Source: U.S. Bureau of Census, Census of Governments, 1967, *Finances of Municipalities and Township Governments.*

Table 3-2
Effective Tax Rates by City

City	"Legal" Effective Rate, 1970	"Actual" Effective Rate, 1966	% Increase in Legal Rate, 1966-70
Atlanta	2.6%	1.9%	29%
Baltimore	3.3%	3.1%[a]	16
Chicago	6.9%	2.5%	27
Detroit	2.8%	2.1%	10[b]
Nashville	2.1%	2.0%	0
Oklahoma City	2.3%	1.8%	0
Philadelphia	2.9%	2.6%	0[c]
Portland	3.0%	2.4%	11
Providence	3.4%	2.9%	13
San Francisco	2.8%	2.5%	N.A.

[a]Based on Baltimore's study of assessment/sales ratio for 31,127 properties of all classes.

[b]Actual rate of taxation has increased by a greater percentage since the assessment/sales ratio has increased.

[c]Large increase in users' taxes.

Notes: The "legal" effective tax rate refers to the legislatively mandated assessment/sales ratio multiplied by the official millage rate for the city. The "actual" median effective tax rate refers to the actual median assessment sales ratio times the official millage rate for the city.

Source: Millage rates and legislatively mandated assessment/sales ratios were obtained from Assessor interviews and verified by reference to appropriate city and state publications. Actual assessment/sales ratios for 1966 were obtained from: U.S. Bureau of the Census, *Census of Governments, 1967, Property Taxes.*

The third column of Table 3-2 shows the percentage increase in the effective property-tax rate between 1966 and 1970. This figure gives some indication of the cities' increasing tax burden, but it tends to understate the rate of increase since certain cities such as Philadelphia have shifted to greater reliance on users' charges during the period. Others, like Detroit, have instituted local income taxes, while still others have raised their actual assessment/sales ratios without revising the legal target ratios.

Compared to the range of effective property-tax rates among all cities, the variation among the sampled cities is relatively small. Among the nation's fifty largest cities, Newark (N.J.) in 1970 had an effective property-tax rate of 8.4 percent while Birmingham (Ala.) had an effective rate of 1.1 percent.

Neighborhood Variation in Tax Rates

The fact that property-tax rates vary among different cities is a direct consequence of the way state and local legislation divides expenditure responsibilities among different levels of government. It also reflects jurisdictional variations in the per capita value of real property as compared with the need for local public services. However, within their boundaries, cities are bound by legislation to tax residential property at a uniform rate of market value, regardless of neighborhood location.[2]

To determine whether, in fact, effective tax rates are equal across neighborhoods, we have classified the sample properties in the four mutually exclusive neighborhood categories described in Chapter 1. These are stable neighborhoods (land and dwelling prices at above-average levels and increasing at the city-wide average); upward transitional neighborhoods (land and property values increasing at a rate above the city average); downward transitional neighborhoods (land and property values declining); and blighted neighborhoods (property values steady at low rates, or sinking toward a zero level).

Table 3-3 reveals that in several cities the effective tax rate varies dramatically among neighborhoods. In Baltimore, Chicago, Philadelphia, and Providence, the neighborhood variation of tax rates in our sample exceeded 500 percent. The tax rates in Table 3-3 have been calculated as the percentage that actual property tax payments represent of investor-reported market value. Reliance on investor reports of the market value of their property introduces random error into a

Table 3-3
Median Effective Tax Rates for Sample Properties by Neighborhood and City for 1970

City	Stable Neighborhood	Upward Transitional Neighborhood	Downward Transitional Neighborhood	Blighted Neighborhood
Atlanta	2.1%	2.1%	2.2%	4.6%
Baltimore	1.6	1.4	9.8	14.9
Chicago	5.2	0.8	4.7	10.7
Detroit	3.1	2.8	3.5	3.0
Nashville	1.5	1.2	1.3	0.9
Oklahoma City	1.5	1.5	2.3	1.7
Philadelphia	1.6	1.0	1.9	9.3
Portland	2.2	2.1	2.6	1.6
Providence	1.2	1.0	–	5.2
San Francisco	2.2	2.0	2.5	1.9
All Cities	1.9	1.4	2.5	3.8
Total Number of Properties	84	96	84	85

Sample: All residential properties reporting estimated market value for 1970.

Notes: Effective Tax Rate is property tax as a percentage of owner-reported market value of the property.

Source: Investor Interview questions 3 and 8, Homeowners Interview questions 6d and 7, and Property Data Sheet question 4.

calculation of this type, but several studies have shown that investor estimates seem to contain no systematic bias toward under- or overestimation of market value compared to actual sales prices.[3] Wherever possible, we corroborated investors' reports of market value with local real-estate experts and recent sales of comparable properties in the neighborhood. The only bias discernible was the tendency of small investors in downward transitional neighborhoods to exaggerate the market value of their properties. In case of serious disagreement, expert opinion on market value was preferred to investors' reports.[4]

The magnitude of variation in neighborhood tax rates is best seen by comparing Tables 3-2 and 3-3. Despite the fact that uniform taxation within each city is mandated by law, the neighborhood variation in several cities exceeds the variation in legal rates adopted by different cities. In Chicago and Baltimore the sample properties in blighted neighborhoods pay property taxes at a rate ten to fifteen times higher than properties in upward transitional neighborhoods. In these cities the regressivity of the property tax's effective rate structure is due principally to neighborhood bias in assessments.

The significance of neighborhood differentials in tax burden may be easiest to grasp in terms of a typical rental payment in a blighted neighborhood. In the blighted neighborhood of East Baltimore, a two-bedroom apartment may rent for $70 per month and command a market price of $1,500. Of the total rent, 20 percent or $14 per month typically goes to pay property taxes. If properties in East Baltimore were taxed at the legally prescribed rate of 3.3 percent of market value, the taxes on this typical dwelling unit would be reduced to just over $4 per month. Passed on to the tenant, the tax savings would represent a *rent reduction* of about 14 percent.

As was discussed in Chapter 2, the extent to which such a rent reduction would actually occur with a reduction in taxability depends on the competitiveness of the housing market. If the owners of housing compete with one another to attract tenants, then eventually the cost reductions achieved by a tax cut will be passed along to the tenant. While the evidence is not conclusive, we will argue in the subsequent neighborhood analysis that housing investors behave more competitively than generally is conceded.

Property Tax Payments as a Percentage of Gross Rent

The residential property tax is designed to be a tax on capital held in the form of residential real estate. In judging the equity of the distribution of tax burdens by neighborhood, the proper comparison is between effective rates of taxation as levied on asset values. These are the figures presented in Table 3-3.

Another measure of tax burden, which may indicate better the role that the property tax plays in housing-market decisions, is given by tax payments as a percentage of gross rents. Table 3-4 displays these percentages for the same city and neighborhood classifications as Table 3-3 does for effective tax rates based on market value. Comparison of the two tables shows that taxes as a percentage of gross rent are much more evenly distributed across neighborhoods.

The reason for the relative equality of taxes as a percentage of gross rent, despite marked differences in tax rates as a percentage of market value, lies in the market's valuation of blighted properties. The cost of operating these properties represents a higher proportion of rent receipts than is true of properties in stable neighborhoods. Therefore, for any given level of gross rent in both types of neighborhoods, net income will be much lower in the blighted neighborhood. Furthermore, the expected duration of this net income flow will be less for blighted properties. In the extreme case of the blighted neighborhoods in Baltimore, Chicago, Providence, or Philadelphia, several investors noted that there was a high probability that in a year or two their properties would be destroyed by vandals or rendered uninhabitable as a result of neighborhood deterioration. Thus the expected lifetime net income of a property was much lower, as a proportion of current rent receipts, than in stable or upward transitional neighborhoods.

Where the net income/rent ratio is low and the prospects are bleak as regards

Table 3-4
Median Tax/Gross-Rent Ratio by Neighborhood and City for 1970

City	Stable	Upward Transitional	Downward Transitional	Blighted
Atlanta	13.4	13.1	13.7	18.7
Baltimore	19.0	9.9	18.0	15.0
Chicago	20.7	9.9	17.4	19.9
Detroit	17.4	11.8	17.5	13.1
Nashville	9.5	7.9	7.8	8.4
Oklahoma City	14.0	8.9	10.8	14.0
Philadelphia	13.2	4.4	6.5	12.1
Portland	16.3	15.0	15.8	11.0
Providence	7.9	7.6	–	20.2
San Francisco	17.8	12.6	16.8	18.4
All Cities	14.4	10.1	12.9	15.5
Total Number of Properties	69	88	74	78

Sample: All residential rental properties reporting gross rent figures for 1970.

Notes: Tax/gross-rent ratio is property tax as a percentage of actual rental receipts. For owner-occupied structures, an imputed rent has been assigned to the owner's apartment on the basis of the rent structure prevailing in the rest of the building.

Source: Investor Interview questions 3 and 12a, Property Data Sheet question 4.

future rental income, real-estate parcels will command relatively low market values compared to their current rental income. In real estate parlance such properties will have a low "gross-rent multiplier." Table 3-5 shows how the market-price/gross-rent ratios or "gross-rent multipliers" were distributed in our sample. Note how much lower the multipliers are for blighted and downward transitional neighborhoods in the four cities where market expectations were poorest.

To demonstrate the importance of the variation in gross-rent multipliers for the distribution of property-tax burdens consider the following identity:

$$T_M = g \cdot T_R$$

where T_M is the property-tax rate as a percentage of market value, T_R is the tax rate as a percentage of gross rents, and g is the gross-rent multiplier or the rate at which total rent receipts are capitalized into market value. Since gross-rent multipliers are highest in stable and upward transitional neighborhoods and lowest in blighted neighborhoods, the variation in g partially offsets the opposite neighborhood variation in effective tax rates based on market value which was shown in Table 3-3. The result is a relatively even distribution of tax/gross-rent ratios.

The relatively equal tax/gross-rent ratios imply that the property tax raises the cost of housing by roughly the same proportion in every neighborhood. If the effective tax rates based on market value had been evenly distributed at the outset, the cost of supplying blighted housing would have shifted less than the

Table 3-5
Median Gross-Rent Multiplier by Neighborhood for 1970

Neighborhood	Median Gross-Rent Multiplier All Cities	Baltimore Chicago Philadelphia Providence	Atlanta Detroit Nashville Oklahoma City Portland San Francisco	Total Number of Properties All Cities
Stable	6.7	6.5	6.8	71
Transitional upward	6.9	7.2	6.8	86
Transitional downward	5.1	3.5	5.9	76
Blighted	4.3	1.5	5.4	72
All neighborhoods	5.8			305

Sample: All residential rental properties reporting rent and value for 1970.
Notes: The gross-rent multiplier is the ratio of the market value of a property to its gross rent receipts.
Source: Investor Interview questions 3, 8, and 12a.

cost of supplying other types of housing, as a result of the imposition of a uniform-rate property tax. That is, property-tax payments as a percentage of gross rent would be less in blighted neighborhoods than elsewhere in a tax system where uniform tax rates are applied to asset values.[5]

As part of the present study, historical data on tax/gross-rent ratios also were gathered. Table 3-6 shows that the relative tax burden of blighted and downward transitional neighborhoods compared to stable and upward transitional neighborhoods has increased substantially over the last five years. In general, property taxes were increasing in all neighborhoods, but in the stable and upward transitional neighborhoods rents were increasing even faster. Thus in the majority of instances in these two types of neighborhood, taxes as a percentage of gross rent declined during the period. The exact opposite was the case in the downward transitional and blighted neighborhoods. There rents typically did not increase as fast as property taxes. As a result, property taxes as a percentage of gross rents tended to increase over the period. In many cases, this increasing burden of property taxation reflects the failure of low-income properties to be reassessed in line with their declining market value as neighborhood conditions decay.

Variation in Tax Rates by Structure and Type

The properties in the sample can be classified in other ways than by neighborhood. Table 3-7 arrays the properties by age of structure and Table 3-8 by size of building. In both cases the range of variation of effective tax rates is much less than when properties are classifed by neighborhood. In fact, what variation there is can be attributed to neighborhood factors. In Baltimore the blighted neighborhood consisted of single-family row houses built fifty years ago. Consequently, Baltimore showed extremely high tax rates in three categories: blighted neighborhood, buildings thirty to sixty years of age, and one-unit dwellings. This predominant importance of neighborhood factors, rather than structural features, is reinforced by Table 3-9. When median effective tax rates are stratified by age of property and neighborhood, the variation in tax rates is much more pronounced across neighborhoods than across age classifications. Within any single neighborhood type the relationship between the age of the building and the effective tax rate is slight, but for buildings of all ages the effective tax rates are consistently highest in the blighted and downward transitional areas.

Incremental Tax Rates on Improvements

According to the legal description of each city's tax system, residential property is supposed to be taxed at a uniform proportion of true value, regardless of date

Table 3-6
Change in Property-Tax Payments as a Percentage of Gross Rent by Neighborhood, 1966-1970

Neighborhood	Number of Properties	Properties for which Taxes as a Percentage of Gross Rent Increased from 1966 to 1970	Percentage of Total	Median Change in Property Tax Payments as a Percentage of Gross Rent 1966-1970
Stable	44	15	34.1%	−1.0
Transitional upward	57	28	49.1	−0.1
Transitional downward	58	40	69.0	+1.6
Blighted	53	35	66.0	+1.8
All neighborhoods	212	118	55.6	+0.7

Sample: All 212 residential rental properties built prior to 1966 for which rent and tax histories could be obtained.

Notes: The difference between property tax as a percentage of gross rental receipts for 1966 and 1970 was calculated for each individual property. The median value of these figures was then selected. A minus figure indicates that tax as a percentage of gross rent declined by one percentage point from 1966 to 1970 (e.g., from 17.0% to 16.0%).

Source: Investor Interview question 12, and Property Data Sheet question 4. Sample: All residential properties reporting estimated market value.

Table 3-7
Median Effective Tax Rates by Age of Building and City, 1970

City	60 Years and Older	15 to 60 Years	Less Than 15 Years
Atlanta	2.3%	2.3%	2.4%
Baltimore	3.9	10.6	—
Chicago	1.5	5.2	—
Detroit	3.3	3.2	3.3
Nashville	—	1.1	1.5
Oklahoma City	—	2.1	1.5
Philadelphia	1.4	1.7	1.6
Portland	2.4	2.3	2.3
Providence	0.9	1.2	1.2
San Francisco	1.9	2.1	2.4
All cities	2.2	2.8	2.0
Total number of properties in sample:	76	156	107

All residential properties reporting estimated market value.

Notes: Effective tax rate payment as a percentage of investor-reported market value of the property.

Source: Investor Interview questions 3 and 8, Homeowner Interview questions 1 and 7, and Property Data Sheet question 4.

Table 3-8
Median Effective Tax Rates by Building Size and City, 1970

City	1 Unit	2-4 Units	5-19 Units	20 + Units
Atlanta	2.3%	3.3%	2.9%	2.1%
Baltimore	9.6	1.9	—	—
Chicago	2.1	1.7	4.7	6.3
Detroit	2.9	3.2	3.2	3.0
Nashville	1.1	1.1	1.2	1.6
Oklahoma City	1.6	2.5	—	1.5
Philadelphia	1.4	2.6	0.9	1.6
Portland	2.4	2.1	1.9	2.5
Providence	1.2	4.1	1.0	1.3
San Francisco	1.8	2.0	2.2	2.3
All cities	2.7	2.5	2.3	2.5
Total number of properties	110	80	72	82

Sample: All residential properties reporting estimated market value.

Notes: Effective tax rate is property tax as a percentage of owner-reported market value.

Source: Investor Interview questions 3 and 8, Homeowner Interview question 7, and Property Data Sheet question 4.

Table 3-9
Median Effective Tax Rate by Age of Property and Neighborhood, 1970

| | Age of Property | | |
Neighborhood	Less Than 15 Years Old	15 to 60	60 And Older
Stable	1.7%	2.1%	1.6%
Upward transitional	1.8	1.9	1.1
Downward transitional	2.1	2.6	3.8
Blighted	4.7	2.2	4.2
All neighborhoods	2.5	2.2	2.4

Sample: All residential rental properties reporting estimated market value.
Source: Investor Interview questions 3 and 12.

of construction. If an improvement to a property augments its market value, this value is to be taxed at the overall tax rate, just as if the value were attributable to the original portion of the property.

In discussions of the property tax, fear of reassessment often is cited as a principal deterrent to upgrading of the housing stock.[6] A tax on the market value of an improvement adds an additional cost which the investor must take into account and consequently reduces the rate of return which he can earn. A 3 percent effective tax rate on market value, when applied to a project that is 90 percent financed by borrowing, reduces an investor's rate of return on equity by 30 percent per annum, unless he can pass the tax on to his tenants. Reductions in profitability of this magnitude are likely to cause investors to forgo many improvements to the housing stock that they would undertake in the absence of reassessment.

The potential disincentive of the property tax is clear. However, the actual disincentive depends on whether improvements to the housing stock in fact result in reassessment. Table 3-10 shows that the proportion of improvements in our sample that were reassessed was surprisingly small. Of all improvements costing less than $10,000 per unit, only 10.3 percent were reassessed within the three years following completion. Of the total 152 cases of private-market rehabilitation examined in the study, only 19 resulted in reassessment over the same period. While it is likely that many more improvements are eventually reflected in assessed valuations—for example, at the time of sale when properties tend to be reassessed to reflect the actual sales value, which in turn reflects any improvements which the owner has made—the property tax's disincentive to improvements in the housing stock seems to have been exaggerated for the simple fact that reassessment occurs only infrequently and with a considerable lag behind changes in market value.

Table 3-11 examines the neighborhood pattern of reassessment of improvements. Among our sample properties, not a single improvement effected by private investors in blighted neighborhoods resulted in reassessment. Typically

Table 3-10
Reassessment of Private-Market Rehabilitation

Value of Rehab	No. of Properties Rehabilitated	No. of Properties Reassessed as a Result of Rehab	Percentage Reassessed
Less than $500	53	1	1.9%
$ 500 to $2,999	62	10	16.1
$ 3,000 to $9,999	30	4	13.3
$10,000 and over	7	4	57.1
All properties	152	19	12.5

Sample: Private market residential structures with any rehabilitation expenditures in the period 1966-1970.
Source: Investor Interview questions 17a, and 20a, Homeowner Interview question 14, 17, and Property Data Sheet question 4.

property values already are overassessed in these neighborhoods, and even major increases in market value leave this situation unaltered. Assessors seem to recognize this fact and refuse to further penalize landlords in blighted neighborhoods by reassessing as a result of repairs of rehabilitation.

The timing of reassessment for improvements varied greatly from city to city. With so few examples of reassessment, few general conclusions can be made. It was apparent, however, that cities such as Portland, which assessed all properties on a regular cycle, often did not reassess smaller rehabilitation expenditures immediately. For these smaller projects, the assessor would wait until the entire neighborhood came up for review and then reassess each building for price appreciation and improvements simultaneously. In other cities, such as Oklahoma City, which do not have a general neighborhood cycle of assessment, reassessment was made within six months of completion of the rehabilitation work. As will be noted in Chapter 9, however, only selected types of rehabilitation expenditures were reassessed at all in Oklahoma City.

Investors' reports tended to confirm that fear of reassessment played a relatively small role in their decision whether or not to make improvements to a parcel. As part of the sample questionnaire, investors were asked to identify what they regarded as the "principal obstacles" to upgrading their property. Table 3-12 presents the response to this question.

As shown in Table 3-12, in only nineteen instances was fear of reassessment listed as the most important obstacle to rehabilitation. Far more important were such reasons as the difficulty in obtaining financing, deterioration of neighborhood quality, or inability to raise rents. The same pattern holds true in Table 3-13, which combines the first and second most important obstacles to rehabilitation cited by investors. Finally, Table 3-14 shows that even among homeowners, fear of reassessment was not considered to be a major obstacle to rehabilitation.

Table 3-11
Reassessment of Private-Market Rehabilitation by Neighborhood

	Less Than $3000 Per Unit			More Than $3000 Per Unit		
	No. of Properties Rehabilitated	No. of Properties Reassessed	Percentage Reassessed	No. of Properties Rehabilitated	No. of Properties Reassessed	Percentage Reassessed
Stable	27	1	3.7%	10	1	10.0%
Transitional upward	26	5	19.2	21	7	33.3
Transitional downward	30	5	16.7	3	0	0.0
Blighted	32	0	0.0	3	0	0.0
All neighborhoods	115	11	9.6	37	8	21.6

Sample: Private-market residential structures built prior to 1961 with any rehabilitation expenditures in the period 1966-1970.

Source: Investor Interview questions 17a, and 20a, Homeowner Interview question 14, 17, and Property Data Sheet question 4.

Table 3-12
Obstacles to Rehabilitation of Rental Properties by Neighborhood (Number of Properties Whose Operators Reported Listed Cause as Most Important Obstacle)

Obstacle	Stable	Upward Transitional	Downward Transitional	Blighted	All Neighborhoods
Difficulty of obtaining financing	17	18	14	24	73
Fear of reassessment	10	4	4	1	19
Deterioration of neighborhood	1	11	21	27	60
Unavailability of labor	3	10	6	3	22
Inability to raise rents	14	3	9	13	39
Does not need rehabilitation	8	8	2	0	18
Other	3	5	6	0	14
Total	56	59	62	68	245

Sample: Private-market residential rental properties built prior to 1961. (Operators of most recently constructed properties mostly reported "does not need rehabilitation".)

Source: Investor Interview question 24a.

Table 3-13
Obstacles to Rehabilitation of Rental Properties by Neighborhood (Distribution of Two Most Important Obstacles)

Obstacles	Stable	Upward Transitional	Downward Transitional	Blighted	All Neighborhoods
Difficulty obtaining financing	22	26	32	34	114
Fear of reassessment	13	8	8	15	44
Deterioration of neighborhood	16	18	26	46	106
Unavailability of labor	11	17	17	6	51
Inability to raise rents	18	6	12	23	59
Does not need rehabilitation	8	8	3	3	22
Other	4	8	10	1	23
Total	92	91	108	128	419

Sample: Private-market residential rental properties built prior to 1961.
Source: Investor Interview question 24a.

Table 3-14
Obstacles to Rehabilitation by Homeowners by Neighborhood (Distribution of Most Important Obstacles)

Obstacles	Stable	Upward Transitional	Downward Transitional	Blighted	Total
Difficulty obtaining financing	5	3	4	5	17
Fear of reassessment	2	0	0	0	2
Deterioration of neighborhood	1	0	2	2	5
Unavailability of labor	1	0	1	0	2
Can't afford the investment	1	0	1	1	3
Does not need rehabilitation	1	1	0	0	2
Other	1	2	1	0	4
Total	12	6	9	8	35

Sample: All single-family owner-occupied homes built before 1961.
Source: Homeowner Interview question 19.

While few investors claimed that fear of reassessment constituted a major obstacle to rehabilitation, future chapters will demonstrate that many investors and homeowners have an unclear conception of how the assessment system functions. Many have expectations of reassessment which, on the basis of assessors' reports and observed assessment practice, are unjustified. Nevertheless, on one point there is fundamental agreement: in practice, reassessment is an infrequent consequence of undertaking improvements and investors perceive it to be a relatively minor obstacle.

4

Blighted Neighborhoods

The underlying reason for the existence of low-quality housing is the disparity between the rents low-income households can afford to pay and the rents required by landlords in order to supply standard housing. In this respect, the consumption of low-quality housing is no different from poor households' consumption of inadequate food, cheap clothing, or other goods and services of low quality. Most low-income families, even spending 30 to 35 percent of their income for rent, simply cannot afford to live in better quality shelter.

The link between low family income and low-quality housing is far too strong to be severed by an alteration in the property tax alone. If society wishes to have its poor citizens housed adequately, it will have to provide them such housing directly, or boost low-income families' purchasing power enough, either through a housing allowance or income supplement, to enable them to purchase standard housing on the private market. However, the purchase of low-quality housing need not bring with it the environment of violence, dismal living conditions and social deterioration that characterizes the "crisis ghetto." Again and again, we found in our sample cities evidence of inexpensive housing being provided in relatively stable low-income neighborhoods. While low-quality housing is not attractive, providing households the opportunity to buy inexpensive housing in a stable environment is a worthy social goal. In this chapter we shall argue that changes in property-tax policy can help to separate the most debilitating effects of the crisis ghetto, from the consumption of inexpensive but physically adequate housing.

The Neighborhood

Low-income neighborhoods have in common poor-quality housing, relatively low property values, and high concentrations of disadvantaged and racially isolated households. As shown in Table 4-1, the concentration of these population subgroups in blighted neighborhoods is associated with a high degree of tenant instability. This tenant instability increased during the 1960s. Table 4-2 shows that one consequence of the recent loss of population in the cities has been the creation of extremely high vacancy rates in the rental stock of blighted neighborhoods. Not only are vacancy rates high and increasing, but the length of time that units remain vacant between rentals often has increased. Finally, there is evidence, summarized in Table 4-2 that the rate of tenant turnover is on the rise.

37

Table 4-1

Tenant Characteristics by Neighborhood

Percentage of Properties With:	Stable	Upward Transitional	Downward Transitional	Blighted
Percentage of tenants less than $5,000 annual income	1%	14%	43%	84%
Percentage of black tenants	19	19	44	80
Percentage of landlords reporting average occupancy of six months or less	2	1	8	19

Sample: All residential rental properties.
Source: Investor Interview questions 6 and 7.

Table 4-2

Selected Aspects of Residential Rental Properties by Neighborhood

Total properties in sample	Stable	Upward Transitional	Downward Transitional	Blighted
Percentage experiencing:				
Increase in vacancy level, 1965-1970	14%	12%	10%	32%
Increase in average period of vacancy 1965-1970	19	14	15	26
Increase in average turnover rate of tenants, 1965-1970	7	9	17	32

Sample: All residential rental properties.
Source: Investor Interview questions 6 and 7.

While blighted neighborhoods share many characteristics, they also differ from one another in significant ways. Table 4-3 presents some salient characteristics of four of the blighted neighborhoods in our sample. Often blighted neighborhoods are portrayed as if they consisted solely of large tenement structures. While this representation of blight adequately describes the situation in some cities, Table 4-3 shows that in the blighted areas of Oklahoma City more than four-fifths of the housing units are single-family structures. High proportions of single-family homes are found in the blighted neighborhoods of Portland (and Atlanta) as well. In contrast, single-family houses account for an extremely small portion of the Chicago and Detroit low-income housing markets. One striking implication of this is the high degree of owner occupancy found in the blighted neighborhoods of Portland and Oklahoma City. This is true even though these two neighborhoods contain populations whose incomes are as low as those living in the other blighted neighborhoods of the sample.

Variations in the housing conditions that exist within blighted neighborhoods

Table 4-3
Characteristics of Selected Blighted Neighborhoods, 1970

City	Number of Housing Units	Percent in Single Unit Structures	Percent Owner-Occupied	Rental Vacancy Rate	Median Contract Rent	Average Value Single-Family Owner-Occupied
Chicago	22,195	4.9%	10.1%	15.6	$112	$18,000
Detroit	13,095	3.6	2.0	16.6*	N.A.	N.A.
Oklahoma City	5,152	80.5	53.0	N.A.	59	10,600
Portland	2,735	41.4	35.3	18.0	62	9,300

*Vacancy rate for Detroit refers to entire housing stock. Given the tendency for the homeowner vacancy rate to be lower than rental vacancy rate, this figure estimates the rental vacancy rate.

Source: 1970 Census Data provided by local city planning agencies. Tracts included in blighted areas, Chicago: 4201 to 4212; Detroit: 24, 25, 29, 30, 31, 32, 34; Oklahoma City: 1013, 1014, 1027, 1028; and Portland: 22.01, 22.02, 23.01, 23.02.

are at least as dramatic as the distinctions among different neighborhoods. In fact, one of the most prominent aspects of the low-quality housing market is the great variety of management styles that appear even on the same block. As is shown in Table 4-1, almost a third of the owners of blighted properties reported that on average their tenants occupied units for periods of six months or less. But another third of owners reported an average occupancy of two years or more. This latter figure compares favorably with the degree of tenant stability in other neighborhoods.

The most important differences that exist within blighted neighborhoods are difficult to convey by statistics alone. In certain areas, despair has set in to such an extent that investors see no possible buyers for their properties, and no way to rid themselves of the continuing cash drain which property ownership represents except through abandonment. In these neighborhoods vandalism and crime often have virtually destroyed the functioning of the housing market. Added to this are the racial antagonism and fears that create conflict between white absentee landlords and an increasingly vocal black tenantry. This combination of events has come to be known as the "crisis ghetto."[1]

In other blighted areas, though the quality of housing is little better and the tenants just as poor, the market in low-income properties remains active. While property values are low, the possibility of resale keeps investors from having the same sense of being trapped into rental management. Rather than abandon their buildings, many owners make marginal improvements to their properties in an effort to hold onto or attract desirable tenants. Those who are able to operate successfully in this market provide reasonably priced low-income housing to a relatively stable tenantry and make a profit as well. In doing so, their actions do much to offset the adverse features of the neighborhood in which they operate.

Given the complex nature of the differences among blighted neighborhoods, these can best be expressed by example:

East Baltimore, located close to the downtown area, was largely a Jewish Community until World War II. At this time the neighborhood began to change over to an almost entirely black population. Up until ten years ago, many investors made good incomes from renting to low-income blacks. Values were strong and there was a market for buying and selling these properties. This situation has changed dramatically. Though the social characteristics of tenants has changed drastically, ownership remains in the hands of whites who now live in other parts of the city. A number of investors indicated that they were afraid to visit their properties. Many of the more stable tenants have moved out of East Baltimore to Patterson Park or to other more desirable areas. Landlords complained of black-white antagonism, vandalism, robberies, and tenants who intimidated older residents. For property owners, all this means that while costs have risen by as much as 50 percent in six years, rent levels have remained almost unchanged. Formerly lucrative investments have become marginal at best. A building in East Baltimore that sold for $4000 to $6000 ten years ago, might now be sold for $500 in cash or $1000 with a minimal down payment. One real estate dealer said that his East Baltimore properties, worth $200,000 in 1955, are worth $30,000 to $35,000 today.

The Pittsburg neighborhood of Atlanta's South Side is in many respects similar to East Baltimore ten years ago. While the neighborhood has for some time housed a low-income black population, investors are still active in the area and continue to maintain their properties. There is, however, a growing uneasiness about crime and a fear of increased tenant destructiveness. Older landlords admit that they find it difficult to deal with their tenants and express a desire to sell their buildings. Unlike East Baltimore, there are buyers for these properties: small real-estate agents, many of them black, who see property ownership as an opportunity to turn hard work and a small amount of capital into an income producing asset. They recognize that low-income housing is a difficult asset to manage, but owing to their ties to the community they feel that they are in a position to satisfy the local demand for modest quality housing. They continue to invest in low-income housing with an eye to cash-flow returns. In many respects, the future of the Pittsburg neighborhood depends on the ability of these new investors to adjust to the changing rental market.

While abandonment and marginal upgrading of housing can and do exist side by side in the same neighborhood, we felt it useful to divide our sample of blighted neighborhoods into two city groups according to the dominant tendency. Four cities whose blighted neighborhoods seem to have reached the terminal stage are Baltimore, Chicago, Philadelphia and—to a slightly lesser extent—Providence. These four cities are the same as those which were grouped together in Chapter 3 as having the most unequal distribution of effective property-tax rates. As will be argued below, the excessive tax burdens on low-income neighborhoods have played a role in the collapse of the low-income housing market in these cities.

The extent of market collapse is indicated in Table 4-4. Nearly two-thirds of the owners in the blighted neighborhoods of the first group of cities expressed a desire to liquidate their holdings immediately, if they could only find buyers for them. To place the numbers in perspective, comparable figures for the remaining cities and neighborhoods have been presented. These show that the phenomenon of the "trapped investor," the man who is holding properties against his will for want of an opportunity to sell out, is concentrated in the blighted and downward transitional neighborhoods of Baltimore, Chicago, Philadelphia, and Providence—where a large proportion of investors face large-scale capital losses on their holdings. In other cities the percentage of investors desiring to sell out was uniformly distributed across housing submarkets.

Many of the respondents who owned property in the blighted neighborhoods of these four cities already had abandoned other residential properties in the same neighborhoods. With no buyers in sight for their current holdings, these investors were reduced to trying to extract whatever quick cash they could get from their holdings, while allowing their buildings to deteriorate. Many foresaw that the process would end in abandonment unless the government intervened to buy the property as part of an urban renewal or highway construction program.

Of course, the mere fact that abandonment occurs does not signify that public policy has failed. Durable goods of all types must be replaced at the end of their useful life and it should occasion no more surprise that houses are

42

Table 4-4
Intention to Sell by Neighborhood and City Grouping Percentage Expressing Desire to Sell Immediately

Neighborhood	Group I (Baltimore, Chicago, Philadelphia, Providence)		Group II (Atlanta, Detroit, Nashville, Oklahoma City, Portland, San Francisco)		Total for All Cities	
	Number of Properties	Percentage Expressing Desire to Sell Immediately	Number of Properties	Percentage Expressing Desire to Sell Immediately	Number of Properties	Percentage Expressing Desire to Sell Immediately
Blighted	31	67.7%	47	27.7%	78	43.6%
Downward transitional	29	65.5	45	24.4	74	40.5
Upward transitional	41	2.4	41	29.3	82	15.9
Stable	25	16.0	62	24.2	87	21.8
All neighborhoods	126	35.7	195	26.2	321	29.9

Sample: All private-market residential rental properties.
Notes: The first group contains those cities with most uneven assessment across neighborhoods.
Source: Investor Interview question 2b, and Homeowner Interview question 3b.

discarded when no longer serviceable than it does that automobiles or airplanes ultimately are scrapped. It is the premature abandonment of still useful housing that represents a loss of social capital. And it is the fact that abandoned units then become a magnet for drug addicts, vandals and other unsavory activities that creates a human tragedy for the households which must remain in such areas.

Respondents emphasized repeatedly that housing abandonment is a neighborhood phenomenon. Once a neighborhood has deteriorated seriously, there is an effective ceiling to the rents that can be charged, regardless of the quality of an individual property. In blighted neighborhoods in Baltimore and Philadelphia this ceiling was about $50-55 per month. From the investor's point of view upgrading units is pointless if there is no way to recover the costs of repairs through increased rents, and neighborhood conditions prevent higher rents from being charged. It is not that the tenants in blighted neighborhoods do not want better housing, but rather that the aspect of improved housing which they value most highly is neighborhood condition. Those who attain greater purchasing power will move to other neighborhoods rather than spend more on housing consumption in the neighborhood where they now live. Once neighborhood blight has progressed to the stage where abandonment begins to occur, costs, too, become a function of neighborhood conditions.[2] Vandalism and theft account for a greater and greater proportion of operating expenses. For several properties in our sample, the annual loss due to vandalism alone exceeded the building's rent roll.

As those who can escape the deterioration of the crisis ghetto move out, landlords are forced to rent to the least desirable segments of the population. These multiproblem households, in addition to being poor, suffer from social pathologies as well. It is the concentration of these pathological poor in particular neighborhoods that signals the point of no return. Crime rates soar, vacant dwellings become havens for drug addicts or gangs of destructive youths. The disintegration feeds upon itself until no part of the area is habitable.

By the time a neighborhood has degenerated to this extent, application of several of the more traditional housing-policy tools may be counterproductive. The enforcement of housing codes, for example, may merely accelerate the abandonment process. The investor then faces the choice of making the expenditures necessary to bring his property up to code standards, and possibly losing this additional investment, or abandoning his property and thereby losing its capital value. If the present capital value is small compared with the expenditures required to satisfy code standards, he may well discover that the optimal strategy is to walk away from the property.[3] Application of rent control measures may have equally disastrous results.[4]

In principle, property-tax policy could also accelerate abandonment. The previous chapter has shown that in several blighted neighborhoods property-tax payments approached 20 percent of gross rent receipts. If the city enforced payment of this tax as long as a property remained in operation, the profitable life of a structure to an owner might fall far short of its economically useful life. At a given level of maintenance costs, the building might produce a 15 percent return on gross rents and still be profitable to operate before property taxes, but still produce a 5 percent cash loss after property-tax payments. If the owner could avoid the tax by abandoning the building, it would be rational for him to do so.

In practice, the property tax did not greatly encourage abandonment in the neighborhoods in our sample because few cities enforced payment of the tax in badly decayed neighborhoods. None of the eleven properties in our sample classified as in imminent danger of abandonment was paying full property tax. Several were paying no tax at all. Four other properties were three years in arrears, the maximum period the city permitted before seizing the property for tax sale. Investors who had abandoned properties reported that their usual procedure was to cease making property-tax payments once these would force them into a permanently negative cash-flow situation. They figured that from this point, they had three to five years to squeeze a positive cash return out of a property if they did not make tax payments, and that it would take the city approximately this long to proceed against them for tax delinquency.

The Housing Market

The abandonment process has received much attention in recent years.[5] This interest was heightened, in fact, by reports that federal housing programs were making the situation even worse.[6] While it is true that under certain circumstances landlords follow a short-term run-down strategy designed to extract the maximum cash flow from a property before abandonment, this type of investment behavior certainly does not typify all blighted area property owners. In fact, Table 4-5 casts serious doubt on the hypothesis that operators in blighted neighborhoods are motivated by significantly shorter-term calculations than real-estate investors in other neighborhoods. From their own reports, the owners of property in blighted and downward transitional neighborhoods would appear to be distinguished from other owners of property by the lower expectation they have of reaping capital gains rather than by the time horizon of their investments. Of course, investors' reports on their own motivation are likely to be unreliable. More trustworthy evidence of investors' long-term intentions in blighted neighborhoods is provided by the surprising extent to which private investors make improvements to their properties. As can be seen from Table 4-6, the frequency of rehabilitation in blighted neighborhoods is only slightly less than that in other neighborhoods. Table 4-7 indicates that many of the improvements in blighted areas represent only marginal upgrading. However, these improvements often represent a substantial investment relative to the purchase price of the property (Table 4-8).

Table 4-5
Primary Investment Objective by Neighborhood

Response Categories—% Answering	Blighted	Downward Transitional	Upward Transitional	Stable
Long-term capital appreciation	17.9%	18.9%	52.4%	39.1%
Long-term rental income	53.8	58.1	23.1	35.6
Short-term capital appreciation	3.8	6.8	7.3	10.3
Short-term rental income	7.7	9.5	8.5	3.4
Tax shelter	3.8	2.7	3.7	4.6
Other	12.8	4.1	4.9	6.9
Total number of properties	78	74	82	87

Sample: Private-market residential rental properties.

Notes: If investor mentions more than one investment strategy, he was asked to rank them according to which strategy he considered to be dominant.

Source: Investor Interview question 2c.

Table 4-9 presents a further breakdown of the privately owned nonsubsidized residential housing stock. All of the residential parcels in the sample were divided into three categories descriptive of the quality of maintenance. Properties were described as (1) quality of housing service being improved, (2) quality of housing service being maintained, and (3) quality of housing service being lowered. Classifications were made from visual inspection of the properties and analysis of the five-year rehabilitation and maintenance histories for each property. While large-scale rehabilitation expenditures raise the quality of housing services provided by a building, there are other ways to upgrade the service level, including more efficient management and better daily maintenance and care of the property. Conversely, properties may be allowed to deteriorate even though some physical improvements are made, for example in response to code violations. Our admittedly impressionistic index of overall housing quality and its direction of change was designed to take into account those aspects of the housing bundle which do not show up clearly in the record of physical improvements reported in Tables 4-6 to 4-8.

As illustrated in Table 4-9 new owners of properties in blighted neighborhoods are far more likely to improve and maintain their buildings than are owners who have held the property for more than five years. The opposite side of the picture, of course, is that the largest number of properties declining in quality are in the hands of owners who purchased them prior to 1966. While less than 20 percent of all buildings in blighted neighborhoods purchased before 1966 were being improved in quality, almost 60 percent of the buildings owned by recent buyers were being upgraded. The frequency of quality decline among old owners was almost five times as great as among new owners.

The above data suggest an important aspect of blighted area submarkets. The investors responsible for upgrading buildings in blighted areas have recognized a

Table 4-6
Frequency of Rehabilitation by Neighborhood and Investor Size, 1966-1970

	Stable		Upward Transitional		Downward Transitional		Blighted		Total	
	Number of Properties	Percentage Rehabbing	Number of Properties	Percentage Rehabbing	Number of Properties	Percentage Rehabbing	Number of Properties	Percentage Rehabbing	Number of Properties	Percentage Rehabbing
Homeowner	13	76.9%	9	66.7%	9	66.7%	9	55.6%	40	67.5%
Investor										
2 to 9 units	3	100.0	10	70.0	9	77.8	7	28.6	29	65.5
10 to 40 units	15	46.7	19	89.5	23	39.1	20	20.0	77	48.1
41 or more units	46	37.0	37	35.1	34	35.3	49	49.0	166	39.8
Total	77	48.1	75	57.3	75	45.3	85	41.2	312	47.8

Sample: Private-market residential structures built prior to 1961.

Notes: Percentage rehabbing gives proportion of the total number of properties in the relevant category with rehabilitation expenditures at any time in the period 1966 to 1970.

Source: Investor Interview questions 3 and 17a; and Homeowner Interview questions 6d and 14.

Table 4-7

Median per Unit Rehabilitation Expenditures by Owner Size and Neighborhood

	Stable	Upward Transitional	Downward Transitional	Blighted	Total
Homeowner	$2600	$4000	$1500	$1500	$2600
Investor					
2 to 9 units	1400	600	1500		800
10 to 40 units	1600	1500	700	500	700
41 or more units	400	1000	400	500	500
Total	1700	2300	800	500	800

Sample: Private-market residential structures built prior to 1961 with rehabilitation expenditures at any time in the period 1966 to 1970.

Notes: Rehabilitation expenditures per unit were rounded to the nearest $100.

Source: Investor Interview questions 3 and 17a, and Homeowner Interview questions 6d and 14.

Table 4-8

Median Rehabilitation Expenditures as Percentage of Market Value of Property by Neighborhood

Investor Size	Stable	Upward Transitional	Downward Transitional	Blighted
Homeowner	18.3	31.4	21.3	13.0
Investor				
2 to 9 units	7.0	31.9	16.5	16.8
10 to 40 units	12.2	22.7	17.3	29.4
41 or more units	13.9	22.8	18.5	20.9

Sample: Private-market residential structures built prior to 1961.

Notes: Percentage rehabbing gives proportion of the total number of properties in the relevant category with rehabilitation expenditures at any time in the period 1966 to 1970. Median per unit expenditures on rehabilitation have been rounded to the nearest $100. For further discussion of percentage maintaining or upgrading their properties see Table 4-7.

Source: Investor Interview questions 3, 17a, and 21; and Homeowner Interview questions 6d, 14 and 18.

diversity of demand for housing that the older owners have failed to perceive. Typically, housing segregation has severely constrained the choice of residential location for black families. As a result, families of widely different incomes and tastes for housing are forced to reside in the same neighborhood. From the point of view of demand, there is no reason why families like these should consume the same quality of housing. Their forced presence in the same neighborhoods creates an opportunity for enterprising entrepreneurs to offer better quality housing at higher prices to some residents and poorer quality housing at lower

Table 4-9
Changes in Quality of the Housing Stock by Date of Purchase and Neighborhood (Percentage Distribution)

Neighborhood	Purchase before 1966				Purchase after 1966			
	Quality Improved	Quality Maintained	Quality Declined	Number of Properties	Quality Improved	Quality Maintained	Quality Declined	Number of Properties
Stable	34.8%	63.0%	2.2%	46	31.0%	69.0%	0.0%	29
Upward transitional	51.2	39.0	9.8	41	52.8	44.4	2.8	36
Downward transitional	19.1	48.9	31.9	47	27.6	44.8	27.6	29
Blighted	18.8	37.5	43.8	64	56.5	34.8	8.7	23
Total	29.3	46.5	24.2	198	41.9	48.7	9.4	117

Sample: Private-market residential rental property built prior to 1961.
Notes: These classifications are based on a visual inspection of the properties and analysis of five-year rehabilitation and maintenance histories for each property. See text for fuller discussion.
Source: Investor Interview question 12, 16, 17a.

prices to others. The investors most likely to respond to this diversity of demand are relatively new owners who remain in close contact with the community and its residents.

Investors who improve their properties to satisfy demand for marginally higher-quality housing in blighted areas tend to follow a common pattern of upgrading. First priority is given to security. Without security protection, the desired tenants cannot be attracted to a building; and without security protection, the other improvements an investor carries out are exposed to vandalism, which reduces their serviceable life to a very short period. Once a building is isolated from its environment, however, internal improvements can be very lucrative. While most of the investment carried out can be classified as "cosmetic" rehab, the term should not carry any derogatory implications. By confining their investment to those improvements which increase a building's rent roll, private investors, in fact, insure that they provide what tenants value most. There is no indication that tenants willingly would pay the cost of bringing a building up to code standards; nor does their limited income allow them to pay the rent increases necessary to make substantial rehabilitation worthwhile; but there is ample evidence that tenants are willing to pay the cost, and more, of certain basic amenities which make living in a dwelling more secure and pleasant.

A good example of an investor who buys up properties in blighted neighborhoods, improves them, and operates them for a new class of tenants is Investor A of Atlanta.

Investor A purchases at low prices structurally sound, distressed properties in Atlanta's Pittsburg neighborhood. One property, acquired by A in 1970 contained four units renting for $55 a month with no utilities. Vacancies had reduced the annual rent roll by nearly 25 percent and the previous owner had operated for several years with a negative cash flow. Mr. A acquired the building for $7,500 by paying $2,500 cash and borrowing $5,000 on a five-year loan. For approximately $800, A built a security fence, painted the apartments, repaired fixtures, and replaced the locks on the doors. Unable to raise the rents, A did manage to reduce vacancies to less than 5 percent in 1970. In addition, A also successfully appealed his assessed valuation, using the purchase price of the property as his main piece of evidence for reassessment. This resulted in a reduction of his property-tax liability from $700 to $500. The combination of these activities have turned a distressed building into an income-producing asset.

Investor A's approach to upgrading his building is typical of blighted neighborhoods in that the principal return on investment often lies in the reduction of vacancies rather than increase in rents. The blighted neighborhoods in our sample had vacancy rates averaging about 15 percent. Many individual buildings had vacancy rates considerably higher. Competition among investors in this situation takes the form of competing for high occupancy rates by increasing the attractiveness of structures to potential tenants. Table 4-10 shows that a

Table 4-10
Result of Rehabilitation by Neighborhood

	Stable	Upward Transitional	Downward Transitional	Blighted	Total
Number of properties	27	41	27	30	125
Rent raised	17	28	11	11	67
Percentage of total	63.0	68.3	40.7	36.7	53.6
Vacancies reduced	3	14	6	15	38
Percentage of total	11.1	34.1	22.2	50.0	30.4
Both vacancies reduced and rent raised	3	12	3	7	25
Percentage of total	11.1	29.3	11.1	23.3	20.0

Sample: All private-market residential rental structures built prior to 1961, with rehabilitation expenditures at any time in the 1966 to 1970 period.

Notes: Rental increase and vacancy reduction must have been the direct result of rehabilitation expenditures.

Source: Investor Interview questions 3, 17a, 22a and 22b.

reduction in the vacancy rate was far more often the consequence of rehabilitation in blighted neighborhoods than it was elsewhere. A reduction in the vacancy rate can have a dramatic effect on a building's cash flow.

Mrs. L. of Detroit purchased a building in 1969 which had eight of its thirty-two units vacant. Though located in a blighted neighborhood, the building was near a hospital. Mrs. L. determined to upgrade the structure in order to attract nurses and paraprofessional staff as tenants. Her investment included the addition of showers to the old-fashioned bathtubs and installation of cheap wall-to-wall carpeting purchased at $1.87 a yard. A wooden fence was placed around the building's parking lot, with a special entry, so that no passage on foot through the street was necessary to enter the building. The result was to reduce vacancies to a single unit and increase per-unit rents by 10 percent. In the first year Mrs. L. increased her *net* cash flow by $12,000 alone from her investment in improvements.

Closely related to this reduction in vacancies is the reduction in tenant turnover and average duration of vacancies that can be achieved with rehabilitation. In spite of increasing vacancy and turnover rates in their neighborhoods, the successful low-income property managers interviewed in our survey were able to find and keep more desirable tenants. Appraisals of "tenant desirability" were not based on a tenant's race, or even his income, but rather on the prospective tenant's ability to make regular rent payments, get along with other tenants and impose low maintenance costs on the dwelling unit he inhabited. Such tenants were viewed as positive assets in a landlord's effort to maintain a viable rental property. By fully renting his units to such tenants, a landlord could significantly reduce loss due to vandalism and theft.

Almost all of the landlords who used minor upgrading to hold onto a stable tenantry were relatively recent purchasers of property who had bought their parcels at depressed prices. Many were area residents. Contrast this managerial style with that of owners who, having purchased or inherited their properties fifteen or twenty years previously, had seen the character of the neighborhood change in a way they did not comprehend. These owners were white. When they first acquired their properties, the residents, too, were white, or, as one respondent put it, a "different kind of black" who was easier for an absentee landlord to deal with. A large number of these owners now are afraid of their tenants and afraid of the prospect of further capital loss on their investment. They wish to sell their properties, but have no offers. The inability to find buyers for the properties has convinced them that it is senseless to put more money into the buildings. Instead, they operate them so as to secure the maximum cash flow possible.[7]

Investor B is a man in his mid-sixties who lives in an upper-middle class section of East Providence. As a child he lived in South Providence, where his father was a small businessman. Late in his life, the father began to buy up a few three-flat wooden frame houses to leave as an estate. B inherited eight of these frame houses. They returned a good, steady income, and B eventually acquired more than 40 of the homes, which by the mid-fifties were worth some $8,000 each. Meanwhile, South Providence began to undergo racial transition. By the 1960s, the area was virtually 100 percent black and had become the city's ghetto. B resents the change in the neighborhood and fears the black tenants he now has. Though his wife protests that it is too dangerous for an old man to visit the neighborhood himself, he collects rents in person on the first and fifteenth of each month, when welfare checks arrive. B wants desperately to sell his properties, but except for an occasional tenant who buys a building on contract, he can find no buyers. Every building he owns, he reports, is for sale at $1,500 and he would accept far less if paid in cash. During 1970, B signed over five of his properties to the city. He wants to donate more, but the city is reluctant to accept them. Meanwhile, B claims to have a negative cash flow in excess of $10,000 per year, even though he owns most of his properties free and clear. His properties have been vandalized repeatedly, and in one, plumbing was stolen three times within eight months. B is determined to invest nothing in his properties except what is demanded by code enforcement officials. When the demands of code enforcement become too severe, he simply offers the property to the city, free.

Mr. B's despair over his neighborhood is typical of many older investors. These owners tended to cite "neighborhood deterioration" as the principal obstacle to upgrading their buildings, as is illustrated in Table 4-11. They also were pessimistic about the chances of raising rents. In contrast, newer investors were more likely to accept the neighborhood as it was. Unlike investors who purchased properties prior to 1966, these new investors did not fear neighborhood deterioration or view the inability to raise rents as an important obstacle to rehabilitation. They saw the possibility of applying sound management, selective upgrading, and careful tenant selection to turn the property into a money-

Table 4-11

Obstacles to Rehabilitation of Rental Properties in Blighted Neighborhoods (Distribution of Most Important Obstacle)

Obstacle	Purchased before 1966		Purchased 1966 or Later	
	Number of Properties	Percentage Distribution	Number of Properties	Percentage Distribution
Fear of reassessment	0	0.0%	1	5.9%
Unavailability of labor	2	3.9	1	5.9
Lack of financing	15	29.4	9	52.9
Deterioration of neighborhood	22	43.1	5	29.4
Inability to raise rents	12	23.5	1	5.9
Total	51	100.0	17	100.0

Sample: Private-market residential rental properties built prior to 1961.
Source: Investor Interview question 24a.

making venture. They realized that most of the neighborhood's decline already was reflected in the level of housing prices. Given an attractive purchase price, they were willing to undertake rehabilitation in order to increase a property's gross rents. The obstacles to upgrading which these investors noted were practical ones, such as the unavailability of financing. They did not doubt the possibility of successfully operating relatively stable low-income housing.

The Role of Property Taxes

Reassessment of improvements plays little or no role in the development of blighted neighborhoods. Information presented in Chapter 3 showed that none of the thirty-seven instances of private rehabilitation undertaken in blighted neighborhoods led to reassessment. The only examples of reassessment as a result of rehabilitation in a blighted neighborhood occurred in nonprofit and government subsidized projects. These will be discussed in a later chapter.

The important assessment issue is rather different in blighted neighborhoods. In most of these areas buildings are overassessed. One of the first actions a knowledgeable purchaser of property in these neighborhoods takes is to appeal his assessment, citing the purchase price of the property as evidence of the lower market value. We found many instances where the annual property-tax reduction, as a result of appeal, was equal to 10 percent or more of the cash equity paid for the structure. This means that the reduced tax liability by itself was enough to give the investor a reasonable rate of return on his investment. One investor in Detroit reported that he deliberately sought overassessed properties for purchase. Typically, the high tax burden of these properties had been capitalized into extremely low property values. By acquiring the property at a low price and obtaining a downward adjustment in assessed valuation, he was able to restore it as a profitable operation and generate for himself a capital gain as well. Unfortunately, relief through the appeals procedure is available in practice almost solely to large investors.

Although the marginal effective tax rate on property improvements is not a significant factor in the operation of housing in blighted neighborhoods, the level of taxation is. This finding is corroborated by other recent studies of the inner city housing market in Baltimore and Newark.[8] For properties in the Newark study that were part of the original sample in 1964, and then restudied in 1971, 48.2 percent of the owners felt that the level of property taxes was the most important inhibitor to housing maintenance. The second most important obstacle was difficulty with tenants (23.4%) followed by the fear of tax reassessment. Yet, only 16.5 percent of the property owners felt that tax reassessment was the most important inhibitor to property upgrading. Among the properties actually abandoned by 1971, the findings are similar. Only 10.2 percent of the respondents felt that tax reassessment was the most important factor. This meant that reassessments were considered a less significant obstacle than the actual level of the property tax (23.4%), tenant problems (45.8%) or building inspection requirements (16.9%).

In addition to affecting the current holders of property, the high level of property taxes contributes to blight in still another way by impeding the transfer of properties from long-time owners who are operating a run-down strategy and want to sell to those investors who are potential purchasers and rehabilitators of slum properties. Low-cost housing is a difficult asset to manage. If the market functioned well, these housing assets would end up in the hands of those people who could operate them most skillfully. As it is, market impediments like the property tax have kept the assets in the hands of those who inherited them and now cannot manage them successfully.

In cities like Baltimore, Chicago, Philadelphia, and Providence, the high level of property taxes substantially reduces operating income on blighted properties. One of the reasons that gross-rent multipliers are so low in the blighted areas of these cities is that the sizeable tax liability that goes with blighted properties sharply reduces their capacity to generate operating income. With operating and maintenance costs accounting for 40 percent of gross rent and property taxes for 17 percent, little is left for amortization, interest on debt, and profit. The lower cash flow is then capitalized into a lower market price.

Continued increases in property taxes can make this situation even worse. Table 4-12 shows that where property taxes, as a percentage of gross rent, have been increasing at the fastest rate, there is the greatest expressed desire on the part of owners to sell properties as soon as they can locate a buyer at what they consider to be a fair price. Most investors who reported that they wanted to sell immediately were long-term property owners in blighted areas; these investors

Table 4-12

Intention to Sell by Change in Property Tax by Neighborhood, 1966-1970

| Neighborhood | Tax as Percentage of Gross Income Increasing, 1966-1970 | | Tax as Percentage of Gross Income Decreasing, 1966-1970 | |
	No. of Properties	Percentage for which Investor Exresses Desire to Sell Immediately	No. of Properties	Percentage for which Investor Expresses Desire to Sell Immediately
Stable	15	53.3%	29	3.4%
Transitional upward	28	14.3	29	6.9
Transitional downward	40	45.0	18	33.3
Blighted	35	45.7	18	22.2
All neighborhoods	118	39.0	94	13.8

Sample: All residential rental properties for which rent and tax histories could be obtained.
Notes: Tax as a percentage of gross income is based on actual rental receipts. For owner-occupied units, an imputed rent has been assigned to the owner's apartment on the basis of the rent structure prevailing in the rest of the building. See also Table 3-6.
Source: Investor Interview questions 5 and 12a; Property Data Sheet question 4.

tend to be victims of the past. They are tied to large capital losses, which they are unwilling to realize by selling at currently depressed prices. Having acquired properties at earlier, higher prices, they often are saddled with heavy debt payments which produce a negative cash flow. When these adverse economic circumstances are combined with social and racial changes which the investors fear, they render owners incapable of looking at their structures as new investment opportunities. While expressing a desire to sell their properties immediately, they often are unable to locate a buyer at what they consider to be a fair price. As Table 4-13 demonstrates, rather than upgrade or maintain their properties, these investors let them deteriorate, hoping to get whatever cash return they can from future urban renewal, highway expansion, or industrial development.

Equalization of tax rates could create an immediate increase in the market value of blighted properties in many cities. On the average these properties are currently paying some 17 percent of gross income for taxes. This could very well be reduced to 10 percent or less, if these properties were taxed at effective rates, based on market value, similar to those found in other neighborhoods of the same cities. Given anything less than a perfectly competitive supply of housing, part of this tax savings will accrue to the landlord as augmented net income. This increment of net income will be capitalized in the property's market value. Lowering property taxes in blighted areas then would allow long-term owners to sell out at a somewhat higher price. By permitting these owners to "bail out"

Table 4-13

Changes in Quality of the Housing Stock by Intention to Sell for Blighted Neighborhood

	Desire to Sell Property Immediately (Percentage Distribution)	No Desire to Sell Property Immediately (Percentage Distribution)
Quality improved	26.5%	30.8%
Quality maintained	26.5	41.2
Quality declined	47.0	25.0
Total number of properties	34	52

Sample: All private-market rental properties built prior to 1961.
Source: Investor Interview questions 12, 16, and 17a.

without the excessive capital losses they want to avoid, the once-for-all price effect of equalizing tax rates might well lead to a large transfer of properties to owners whose ability to manage blighted properties is greater.

To the extent landlords in blighted areas would pass on to tenants the cost savings resulting from tax equalization, tenants would benefit directly. As was discussed in Chapter 2, whether this occurs or not depends on the competitiveness of housing supply. Evidence gathered for this study suggests that blighted-area housing markets may be quite competitive. In Providence we determined the ownership of 2476 properties in each of four assessor's districts. Two of the districts were upward transitional neighborhoods, one was blighted, and one downward transitional. Table 4-14 reveals the extensive fragmentation of ownership in each of the three housing submarkets. In the blighted neighborhood, only six individuals owned five or more properties. The largest owner had only eighteen parcels, many of which were vacant lots.[9]

The lack of concentration of ownership in the low-income housing market in Providence clearly contradicts the image of a housing market dominated by several large slum lords. In other cities, the large slum lord was often talked about, and certainly individuals who own several thousand units exist, but in each city we also found and talked to large numbers of smaller investors in blighted areas, including many black real-estate operators, who specialized in buying and managing a limited number of low-income properties. While this topic deserves additional study, we conclude that there is considerable evidence that low-income areas are not the sole province of few large investors.

Conclusion

This chapter has highlighted the role that property taxes can play in the disintegration of the housing market in low-income areas. Given the difficulty of

Table 4-14
Ownership Patterns in Four Providence Neighborhoods

	Total Number of Projects	Total Number of Property Owners	Owners of Only One Property	Owners with 2 to 4 Properties	Owners with 5 or More Properties
Upward transitional (Plat 15)	464	121	95	22	4
Upward transitional (Plat 16)	599	316	263	48	5
Downward transitional (Plat 69)	643	309	265	41	3
Blighted (Plat 23)	770	408	326	76	6
Total	2476	1154	949	187	18

Source: Survey data collected from assessment records, Office of the Assessor, Providence, Rhode Island.

dealing with multiproblem, low-income households, the management of low-income housing is a difficult task at best. If management fails, stable low-income households will move out of an area. Our interviews identified the existence of a class of property owners and managers who were able to successfully operate under these difficult conditions. If the low-income housing stock can be transferred to those who are most capable of managing it, there is an opportunity to stabilize blighted areas.

The role the property tax plays in this market was somewhat unexpected. We found no support for the contention that the property tax significantly discourages marginal upgrading of blighted properties. In practice, we found no examples of reassessments occurring as a result of property improvement. However, the higher rate of property taxation in blighted neighborhoods has done much to drive up operating costs and depress housing prices. For this reason, it has contributed measurably to the sense of despair that pervades the crisis ghetto. If cities would follow their legal mandate to uniformly assess all residential properties, irrespective of neighborhood location, the resulting once-for-all tax relief that accrued to blighted parcels would probably encourage a large-scale transfer of properties by current owners who had a chance to recoup a portion of their capital losses. Evidence was cited in this chapter that such an ownership transfer would improve the quality of the low-income housing stock.

Social and physical decay need not characterize all low-income areas. The existence of many stable low-income housing markets points to the possibility that low-income housing can be disassociated from the environment of violence and fear that often accompany it. Reform of property assessment practices can substantially increase that possibility.

5 Downward Transitional Neighborhoods

The problems of downward transitional neighborhoods are in many ways representative of the overall problems confronting the center city. The facts of an aging housing stock, the growing exodus of a white middle-class population, and the increased concentration of the old, the poor, and the disadvantaged in the central-city neighborhoods are all too common. The role that property taxation can play in the dynamics of downward transition will be investigated in this chapter. The discussion will first present a brief outline of several of the neighborhoods included in our survey. It will then proceed to outline the major issues delineated by investors in response to our questions regarding the role that property tax plays in the declining neighborhood. Finally, the discussion turns to an analysis of neighborhood efforts to arrest the downward spiral, and to the role that local and federal officials can play in assisting these efforts.

The Neighborhood

Several downward transitional neighborhoods in our sample were in the process of racial succession. Some respondents felt that the downward transition was caused by the influx of blacks or other minorities into an area. Others pointed to the fact that the decline in the quality of housing in the neighborhood was well advanced prior to the in-movement of minorities. Both explanations do injustice to the dynamics of downward transition, as the example of the Logan Square area of Chicago will demonstrate.

Located in the Near North West side of Chicago, the Logan Square area developed rapidly at the turn of the century following the extension of the elevated train service. At first the home of Germans and Norwegians, by 1930 the area's population of 114,000 was a mixture of many ethnic groups. While some structures date to the 1800s, much of the stock was built during the 1920s. As the 1960 census reported, less than 1 percent of the area's stock was built in the 1940-60 period. The curtailment of new building activity was reflective of the general stagnation of the area. Since the 1930 peak, the population has declined gradually to the 1970 level of 94,000. While for many years the decline of the neighborhood was often imperceptible, recent developments have changed this. The expansion of low-income black areas south of Logan Square has alarmed many local residents. The principal fear is that the social disruption, violence, and blight of these areas will soon spill over into their own neighborhood. In addition, both blacks and Puerto Ricans have been moving into Logan Square. While most investors interviewed admitted that these families often had higher incomes than the current white population, they felt that this was only the forerunner of the movement of low-income blacks into the neighborhood. It is this overwhelming fear of ghetto expansion, and the related fear of future capital loss, that dominated the actions of the investors in the area.

While similar fears were expressed by property owners in other racially transitional neighborhoods, there were important examples of neighborhood decline that did not involve the element of racial succession.

The Brooklyn area of Portland was once a solidly middle-class neighborhood of single-family houses. As incomes increased, many people moved out of the area in search of larger and newer housing. Those who remained were often unable to afford to rent or purchase homes of the size that were available. Seeing this possibility, small investors had converted many homes into duplexes and rented them out. While there is some new construction and speculation in land prompted by the neighborhood's attractive location, for the most part, the neighborhood is gradually showing the signs of age and deterioration.

In the Capital Hill area of Oklahoma City this process of gradual decline is well advanced, Single-family homes and duplexes that had been poorly constructed forty years ago are now near the end of their economic usefulness. While not as pleasing to the eye as some of Oklahoma City's newer areas, Capital Hill provides cheap rental housing and home ownership at prices that even the city's poorest families can afford.

The Housing Market

While each of these neighborhoods is unique in many ways, they have in common a past history of declining property values and uncertain expectations regarding future market values. In the extreme case of the Logan Square area, skilled investors felt there was a high probability that property values would decline dramatically in the next five years. Consider the case of a large investor in the area.

Mr. R purchased a fifty-unit building in the Logan Square area in 1966 by assuming a $70,000 mortgage and paying $140,000 cash. The building was poorly maintained and Mr. R put little into the property. In 1969 Mr. R was confronted with increased vacancies and rapidly declining cash flow. At this stage Mr. R decided to test the possibility of rehabilitating his building. For $3000, he upgraded one of his units and increased the rents by $648. Moreover, the rehabilitation expenditure was eligible for an accelerated depreciation over a five-year period, giving the project an additional $300 annual return for the first five years in the form of tax savings. Despite the apparent success of this experiment, Mr. R decided not to upgrade the building. In his opinion, if the blighted area did spill over into Logan Square, it would be difficult, if not impossible, to continue to find tenants who would be willing to pay the higher rents. In addition, there was a high probability that tenant vandalism, so common in blighted areas, would destroy his improvements. Whether through economic conditions or physical destruction, Mr. R viewed the possible loss of an additional $150,000 investment as unacceptable. Instead of rehabilitation, he made some minor repairs and hoped he could hang onto the building for two more years to get the maximum tax shelter advantage of the original investment. In the meantime, he was looking for a new buyer and would consider any sale which might cut his losses. He indicated a tremendous fear that if he did not sell soon enough, he would be forced to hold the property indefinitely.

The realization that downward transition, once under way, usually culminates in blight, deters further investment in the housing stock in these neighborhoods. Investors feel they cannot recover at time of sale even a part of the costs of substantial improvements. In the face of such risk, large investors begin to look for investment opportunities in other neighborhoods. Mr. R, for example, is currently involved in the rehabilitation of a twelve-unit apartment building in Lincoln Park's upward transitional neighborhood in Chicago. As is typical of such neighborhoods, the building has a low effective tax rate. Mr. R felt it was unlikely that the building would be reassessed even after substantial rehabilitation. These features heightened the attractiveness of the project.

The movement of investment capital out of a downward transitional neighborhood helps to insure that the worst expectations of the large investor are met. The ability of the neighborhood to maintain a middle-income population of any mix is eroded by the failure of large numbers of investors to risk additional investments in their buildings. As these buildings deteriorate, it becomes increasingly difficult to rent them to anyone but the low-income people moving in from the nearby blighted neighborhood.

To this point, the discussion has relied almost entirely on opinions and information gathered during interviews with skilled, professional real-estate investors. Much of the real estate in these neighborhoods, however, is owned by owner-occupants and small investors. As Table 5-1 demonstrates, in cities such as Chicago, Detroit and Providence, nearly 40 percent of all rental units in multiple-family dwellings are in owner-occupied structures. In many older ethnic areas of the city, the percentage of rental stock in owner-occupied buildings exceeds the city-wide average given in these tables. The small owner-occupant of a two- to ten-unit building is the dominant investor type in such areas.

Also of interest is the dramatic change in the pattern of owner-occupied housing. In 1960, for example, there were 32,720 rental units in owner-occupied multi-family buildings in Baltimore. By 1970 this number had declined to only 16,735. For Detroit the figures were 51,356 in 1960 and 65,246 in 1970.[1] Although both cities experienced substantial racial transition during this decade, in other respects they were markedly different. For instance, the number of absentee-owned buildings grew steadily in Baltimore, while in Detroit the number declined.

The owner-occupant, then, is an important factor not only in the single-family housing market, but as a supplier of rental housing. On the basis of our

Table 5-1

Distribution of Rental Housing Units in Multiple Structures, 1970 (By City)

City	In Owner-Occupied Multiple-Unit Structures	Total Rental Units in Multiple Structures	Owner-Occupied Multiple Units as Percentage of Total
Atlanta	7,624	75,673	10.1%
Baltimore	16,678	96,410	17.3
Chicago	260,906	703,979	37.1
Detroit	65,246	168,578	38.7
Nashville	6,723	36,112	18.6
Oklahoma City	3,533	23,114	15.2
Philadelphia	43,186	181,040	23.9
Portland	7,403	42,746	17.3
Providence	15,365	38,422	40.0
San Francisco	37,275	174,357	21.4

Source: U.S. Bureau of the Census, Census of Population and Housing, 1970, *Detail Housing Characteristics, United States Summary*, Table 39.

sample, there is reason to believe that owner-occupants in the downward transitional neighborhoods maintained their property at a higher quality level and spent more on rehabilitation than absentee owners. Thus the prospects for arresting the downward transition of the quality of the housing in a neighborhood may very well depend on keeping the small owner committed to his property.[2] It is essential, therefore, to understand his mode of operation.

Investor J purchased his three-flat apartment building for $21,500 in 1964. Although it was nearly sixty years old, the building was structurally sound and for the most part well-maintained. J lived in one unit and rented two other two-bedroom apartments for $80 and $90, unfurnished with no utilities included. The owner stressed the fact that the annual rent of $2040 nearly covered payments on interest and principal of $1380, property taxes of $538, insurance of $137, and water payments of $40 (total $2095). This fact insured that even in time of unemployment or family crisis, the investor would be able to hold onto his home.

In addition, the owner felt that the security of owning property was enhanced by a sound policy of preventive maintenance and gradual upgrading. Staying ahead of repairs not only provided him with better housing today; it was also seen as a way of forestalling future difficulties. A well-maintained house could go for some time without much maintenance if the owner were temporarily unable to afford such expenses in the future. Investor J was a lifelong resident of the area, and no doubt the wave of foreclosures that swept the area in the 1930s had made a lasting impression on his mind.

Another element in the strategies of the small investors interviewed is their view of real estate as a vehicle for wealth accumulation.

Mr. S, a man in his late sixties from the Brooklyn neighborhood of Portland, purchased his first building in 1950 on contract. In 1956 he refinanced that building and used the money to purchase two additional properties. Now he owns sixteen units valued at more than $50,000. Upon retirement, he plans to gradually sell off his holdings.

Mr. and Mrs. M sold their duplex in Logan Square, Chicago and used the money to make a sizable downpayment on a seven-unit building. While running a cash loss on the building, they are optimistic that once the mortgage is paid down, they will reap returns in the form of both cash flow and their ability to borrow against the property.

Typically, the upgrading of owner-occupied structures involves a limited cash expenditure and a liberal expenditure of the owner's time and effort. The cases of two property owners in East Detroit provide examples.

Mrs. A estimated that she and her husband had put some $3000 worth of work into improving a recently purchased duplex. He was able to do minor electrical, plumbing, and carpentry repair work, while she prided herself on being a skilled painter, tile worker, and general carpenter's helper. The cash requirements for their efforts were approximately $600.

Mr. P, a man in his forties, recalled that ten years ago, when he first purchased his duplex, he could hardly change a light bulb. When confronted with increasing maintenance problems, and mindful of the increased costs of hiring repairmen, he soon learned how to do most minor repairs. Most recently, he had finished the construction of a small garage, a clear indication of the degree to which his skills had advanced.

The maintenance and upgrading of properties was found to be a key element in the strategy of many small investors and owner-occupants. As noted in Table 5-2, a greater percentage of small investors did rehabilitation work than was true of the larger investors in the downward transitional neighborhoods. If the dollar value of the owners' labor is included in the cost of rehabilitation, it is the small investors who tended to spend more per unit.

Table 5-2 also presents similar figures for the homeowners in the downward transitional neighborhoods. Like the small investors, the homeowner often does much of his own maintenance and repair work. Through a combination of their own labor and cash expenditure, many homeowners in our sample were able to significantly upgrade their own housing.

The next to last column of Table 5-2 demonstrates that not only did large owners fail to upgrade their properties, but that in many instances the quality of their structures was declining. This reflects the reluctance of individual large investors to risk additional expenditure in the downward transitional neighborhood.

The phenomenon of well-maintained owner-occupied structures existing side by side with deteriorating structures owned by large investors was a point frequently made by small investors and homeowners in these neighborhoods. Indeed, in all the neighborhoods in our sample, owner-occupants and homeowners were more likely than absentee owners to be maintaining and upgrading their properties.

Table 5-3 documents the impressive amount of upgrading of owner-occupied structures found in all of the neighborhoods sampled. Even in the blighted neighborhood, owner-occupants were more likely to maintain and upgrade their properties.

As noted earlier, in the blighted neighborhoods of Oklahoma City, Nashville, Atlanta, and Portland, single-family detached structures predominate. Despite the low incomes in these areas, there is a surprising amount of homeownership. Given the maintenance and rehabilitation record of the owner-occupants who were interviewed, the encouragement of additional homeownership in these neighborhoods could result in considerable upgrading of the housing stock. In the older ethnic areas in the stages of decline, a similar beneficial effect would result from the maintenance of the high level of owner-occupancy already found in these areas.

While pride of ownership on the part of owner-occupants is an important element in maintaining the quality of the housing stock, several problems associated with owner-occupancy need to be mentioned. Older owner-occupants

Table 5-2
Distribution of Rehabilitation Activity by Size of Investor for Downward Transitional Neighborhoods

Size of Investor	Total Number of Properties	Percentage Rehabbing	Median Per Unit Expenditures on Rehabilitation	Percentage Maintaining or Upgrading Their Properties	Percentage Using Borrowed Funds
Single-family homeowners	10	60.0%	$1,500	100.0%	0.0%
Investors with:					
2 to 9 units	9	77.8	1,500	89.9	28.6
10 to 40 units	23	39.1	700	73.9	11.1
40 or more units	34	32.4	400	52.9	9.1
Total	76	43.4	800	69.7	12.1

Sample: Private-market residential structures built prior to 1961.

Notes: Percentage rehabbing gives proportion of the total number of properties in the relevant category with rehabilitation expenditures at any time in the period 1966 to 1970. Median per unit expenditures on rehabilitation have been rounded to the nearest $100. For further discussion of percentage maintaining or upgrading their properties see Table 4-7.

Source: Investor Interview questions 3, 17a, and 21; and Homeowner questions 6d, 14, and 18.

Table 5-3
Maintenance and Rehabilitation Activity of Owner-Occupants by Neighborhood

Neighborhood	Total Number of Properties	Percentage Rehabbing	Median Per Unit Expenditures on Rehabilitation	Percentage Maintaining or Upgrading Their Properties	Percentage of Rehabilitation Projects Financed
Stable	20	65.0%	$2,500	100.0%	65.0%
Transitional upward	20	80.0	3,100	90.0	43.8
Transitional downward	16	68.6	1,500	100.0	18.2
Blighted	12	50.0	1,000	66.7	50.0
Total	68	67.7	2,000	91.7	47.2

Sample: Private-market residential structure built prior to 1961.

Notes: Percentage rehabbing gives proportion of the total number of properties in the relevant category with rehabilitation expenditures at any time in the period 1966 to 1970. Median per unit expenditures on rehabilitation have been rounded to the nearest $100. For further discussion of percentage maintaining or upgrading their properties, see Table 4-7.

Source: Investor Interview questions 3, 17a, and 21; and Homeowner Interview questions 6d, 14 and 18.

in downward transitional neighborhoods may have lost much of their ability to maintain their properties. Forced to pay cash for repair work, they lose one of the significant advantages of owner-occupancy.

As both the housing stock and the population of the neighborhood age, deterioration of the owner-occupied stock may become an important neighborhood problem. These older owners are often reluctant to go into debt to finance needed repairs and feel uneasy about dealing with contractors and hired repairmen. As one older woman who owned a small rental unit observed, "The property will last for my lifetime, and that's good enough for me." A well-maintained house will hold up with minimal maintenance for some time, and this seems to be the rationale of many older homeowners.

Other instances of the decline of maintenance on the part of owner-occupants were found in neighborhoods in racial transition. Several owner-occupants admitted that they were holding back on needed repairs because they were afraid that the growing number of minority people in the neighborhood would force them to leave the area.

The Impact of the Property Tax

In the downward transitional neighborhood, it is the expectations of future market conditions that most influence investor activity. To the extent that the equalization of effective tax rates across neighborhoods improves the market situation in the blighted areas, it also improves the expectations of investors in the downward transitional neighborhood. Not only would such flexibility in assessments alleviate somewhat the cash-flow squeeze that forces many investors to defer necessary maintenance, it would also enhance the expected sale price of any property. Both would increase the possibility that large investors would respond to the current demand for improved housing, rather than withdraw from the area in fear of future market collapse.

To the small investor the importance of property-tax policy is quite different. Often, in the downward transitional area, small owners were unaware of adverse market trends. When asked to discuss the current market value of their property, such owners frequently cited their purchase price or made reference to the current assessed value of their property. Only in certain instances was the small investor able to cite the sale prices of comparable properties.

Given small investors' reliance on assessed valuation as an indication of property values, if reassessment lags far behind market trends, there will be a resultant lag in investors' awareness of the declining value of their property. Consider the example of the downward transitional neighborhood in the early stages of racial transition. The Logan Square area had been gradually deteriorating for decades but assessments had not been reduced accordingly. Recently, increased numbers of Puerto Ricans and blacks moved into the area. One large realtor noted that it was racial change that brought the first awareness of neighborhood decline to many of the members of the community. Owners who previously paid little attention to the market situation, suddenly began to follow closely the sale price of housing in their neighborhood. It is at this time that the false expectations are shattered. This in turn can help to promote the impression that the decline in observed sale price is caused by the presence of minority buyers. The rapid decline in expectations concerning the neighborhood may become a crucial element in the panic selling that often sweeps such neighborhoods.

A further indication of the importance of assessment in such situations was the attempt by a group of black and white citizens to prevent the assessor from reducing the assessed valuation of properties in a racially changing neighborhood in North East Oklahoma City. While there have been some panic sales and a brief period of depressed prices, they are now stabilizing. The neighborhood group argued that the housing stock was new, well maintained, and would sell in the near future for prices comparable to those charged prior to the panic. To reassess downward on the basis of declining market values could very well shatter the confidence in the neighborhood held by those who decided not to sell in the face of social transition.

This effort of a group to raise their taxes is a striking example of the importance that assessments can have in shaping neighborhood attitudes. Many Oklahoma City communities had not had a general reassessment for eighteen years; any reassessment was taken to be a sign of major importance. In Chicago the failure of periodic reassessments to accurately reflect market decline gave small investors an inflated sense of the value of their property. Both examples point to the importance of periodic reassessments. While the assessor cannot be expected to adjust to every fluctuation in sales, reassessment should roughly follow the trend of the market and should be carried out frequently enough to prevent a major change in assessment from sending a shock wave through the neighborhood.

The nonprofessional small investor not only lacks an accurate impression of trends in prices in the neighborhood, he often has a very hazy idea of how the assessments are determined. As noted in Table 5-4 only 15.2 percent of all buildings rehabilitated or upgraded in the downward transitional neighborhood were reassessed. Of those buildings reassessed, in no instance was the increase in assessment more than 20 percent of the dollar amount of rehabilitation expenditures. Despite these facts, many investors felt that any rehabilitation expenditure would lead to reassessment. While this fear of reassessment was not cited as a major obstacle to rehabilitation by investors, this misunderstanding of the workings of the property-tax system needlessly adds risk and uncertainty to many investment decisions. Consider investor J from Logan Square again. As part of his strategy of staying ahead of repairs, he had put new siding on his building. He claimed he was reassessed upward and noted that next time he would know better than to improve the exterior of his building. In fact, the

Table 5-4
Reassessment of Rehabilitation in Downward Transitional Neighborhoods

Per Unit Expenditures	No. of Properties Rehabilitated	No. of Properties Reassessed as a Result of Rehab	Percentage Reassessed
$ 0 to $ 499	12	0	0.0%
$ 500 to $2999	18	5	27.8
$3000 and over	3	0	0.0
All properties	33	5	15.2

Sample: Private-market residential structures built prior to 1961 with any rehabilitation expenditures in the period 1966-1970.

Notes: See Tables 3-10 and 3-11 for comparison of reassessment of neighborhoods.

Source: Investor Interview questions 17a, and 20a; Homeowner Interview question 14, 17 and Property Data Sheet question 4.

marginal increase in assessment was one that was applied to every three-flat apartment building in the neighborhood.

As will be discussed in Chapter 9, many large investors shared this mystification about the assessment process. In Atlanta a large real-estate operator confessed that he had been in the business for fifteen years and still could not predict whether or not a particular rehabilitation would be reassessed. The assessor claimed to check out large building permits, but since the dollar estimates on building permits were often unreliable, the assessor obviously had some additional rules for selecting which buildings to inspect. In repeated efforts, this investor had not been able to obtain a clear statement as to the procedure used.

Although many investors in the downward transitional neighborhoods have little understanding of market and assessment practices, they are acutely aware of the increased tax burden they are forced to bear. The increase in taxes relative to rent generating ability demonstrated in Table 5-5 has seriously eroded the benefits of holding real estate in these neighborhoods. This is especially true for the small investor. Again consider Investor J.

For the present, Investor J felt that there was a secure balance between his cash rent receipts (rents excluding an imputed rent for his own unit) and what he felt were the fixed costs of property ownership—taxes, debt service, insurance, and city-service collections. His taxes had roughly doubled in five years. If they doubled again in the next five years, and if he were unable to increase his rent roll, which is likely, this investor could be spending out of pocket to make up the difference between cash rent and fixed costs. After necessary maintenance costs have been incurred, this property could still have a positive rate of return in a strict accounting sense (i.e., if there were an imputed rent charged the owner for his own lodgings), but the main security element of property ownership has been threatened.

Table 5-5
Change in Property Tax as a Percentage of Gross Rent by Neighborhood

Neighborhood	Number of Properties	Properties for which Taxes as a Percentage of Gross Rent Increased from 1966 to 1970	Percentage of Total	Median Change in Taxes as a Percentage of Gross Rent 1966-1970
Stable	44	15	34.1%	−1.0
Transitional upward	57	28	49.1	−0.1
Transitional downward	58	40	69.0	+1.6
Blighted	53	35	66.0	+1.8
All neighborhoods	212	118	55.6	+0.7

Sample: All 212 residential rental properties built prior to 1966 for which rent and tax histories could be obtained.

Notes: The difference between property tax as a percentage of gross rental receipts for 1966 and 1970 was calculated for each individual property. The median value of these figures was then selected. A minus figure indicates that tax as a percentage of gross rent declined by one percentage point from 1966 to 1970 (e.g., from 17.0% to 16.0%).

Source: Investor Interview question 12; and Property Data Sheet question 4.

To the extent that the small investor provides much of his own management and maintenance, he is protected from certain aspects of the cost squeeze encountered by many holders of real estate who are forced to contract out maintenance and repair work at ever increasing wage levels. To such an owner, property tax is often the most visible and most bothersome of his increasing costs. Under favorable conditions, owner-occupants were able to turn hard work and minimal cash requirements into both a secure home for their families, and hopefully, a small amount of wealth for their later years. In the downward transitional neighborhood these advantages are gradually being reduced. Given the decline in property values, the rise in property taxes is often excessive. A periodic reassessment downward would greatly enhance the ability of a given set of owner occupants to hold onto their properties, and the ability of new owners to come into the area. While it is not possible to say that property-tax increases are the cause of neighborhood decline, once neighborhood decline is underway, a tax system that neither responds to market changes nor is well understood by so many small investors can seriously erode one of the major strengths of the neighborhood—the commitment of many owner-occupants and small investors to their neighborhood and to their homes.

Reversing Downward Transition

Atlanta's West End neighborhood illustrates the role that government intervention can play during a crucial stage in neighborhood transition.

The West End neighborhood of Atlanta is a curious mixture of an old, closed-in neighborhood and a lower-density single-family area. While much of the housing stock dates to the turn of the century, as Atlanta grew in the post-World War II period, some new construction found its way into the West End in the form of new single family homes and low-density apartment development. Despite this, the West End steadily lost ground to the more dynamic and affluent sections of North Atlanta. By the early 1960s much of the stock was seriously deteriorating. To remedy this situation, West End Urban Renewal Area was established to administer a program of federally subsidized loans and grants for rehabilitation, as well as to stimulate new housing and commercial investments. The activity generated by the program is impressive. A new shopping mall is rapidly approaching completion. Other commercial facilities have been upgraded. With the initial round of federally subsidized loans and grants nearly exhausted, the neighborhood faces the crucial test of demonstrating that the downward decline has, in fact, been arrested.

The West End, then, had been declining for years. Many owner-occupants through inability caused by old age, or lack of confidence in the neighborhood resulting from their fear of racial change, were neglecting their properties. The choice of this neighborhood for a program of code enforcement and widespread utilization of federally subsidized home-improvement loans and grants was timely. It did not reverse the course of racial transition—the neighborhood is now 70 percent black. It did stimulate rehabilitation activity. In doing this, the program helped ensure that during the difficult period of racial succession, neighborhood deterioration did not accelerate.

By now the new nature of the neighborhood is becoming clear to residents and investors alike. With a mixture of middle-income whites and blacks committed to the idea of preserving the West End as a healthy, integrated neighborhood, there is reason to believe that the decline has been reversed. This reversal of expectation is best demonstrated by the privately financed construction and rehabilitation of apartment units to serve the expanding middle-income black population.

The West End of Atlanta gives a clear example of how the worst expectations of large and small investors about the future of a neighborhood can be reversed. While the key in Atlanta was the timely utilization of a program of loans and grants, the important role that tax policy has to play in such a neighborhood should not be overlooked. As the next section will illustrate, the success of various federal housing programs is intricately related to local assessment practices.

The Property Tax and
Federally Subsidized Housing

The discussion of the private market in the last two chapters may have obscured the fact that most current investment in the housing stock of blighted and downward transitional neighborhoods is federally subsidized. Rehabilitation under Section 236 of the 1968 Housing Act by itself accounts for a substantial proportion of all investment in these neighborhoods. No less than 88 percent of the total dollar value of rehabilitation in the blighted and downward transitional neighborhoods of our sample came from 236 rehab projects. These projects now dominate investment in multiunit stock in blighted areas; yet no federal policy exists as to how these projects should be taxed. Assessors in two cities identified the lack of federal guidelines on how to assess 236 projects as among the most urgent policy problems they confront. Without exception, investors in these projects reported that the uncertainty surrounding property-tax liability was a principal obstacle to their planning and operation. The matter at stake is important, for how the property tax is administered affects the volume of federally assisted projects undertaken in a city and helps to determine how successful a program is in reducing rents for low-income families.

Assessment of Subsidized Projects

The great dilemma in assessing federally assisted housing projects is that the "value" of these projects is inherently ambiguous. Construction costs are known; but these overstate the market value of a project, since in the absence of subsidy the rental stream produced by the property would not justify the actual expenditure on construction.

The cost of rehabilitation under a Section 236 program may exceed $2 million, yet the resale value of this same project, if sold on the free market without its federal subsidy, may be zero, or even negative in the event that annual unsubsidized costs exceed market rent. Should the local taxing authority then enter the project on its tax rolls at the cost of $2 million? At the assumed free-market value of zero? Or should it apply some other criterion, such as a percentage tax on gross rents? In the absence of plain reasons for preferring one assessment basis to another, cities have vacillated among various formulas for taxing 236 and 221(d)3[1] projects. The result is that it has become extremely difficult for operators of projects to predict their tax liability into the future. The chance that the assessor will change the standard of assessment, thereby substantially augmenting a property's tax liability, adds significantly to the risk of operating 236 and 221(d)3 projects. These projects are so highly leveraged that a change in property taxes can easily convert a project with a significant positive rate of return into one with a negative cash flow.

Nonprofit organization A in Atlanta operates a 280-unit 221(d)3 project for low-income families. A two-bedroom apartment rents for $72.50 per month. The respondent reported that in his judgment "the City is eating up the federal housing program through property taxation." The building sponsored by A was assessed at $568,000 in 1965, its first full year of operation. In 1966 the assessment was jumped to $790,000. After appeal, it was lowered in 1967 to $501,000. These erratic movements in assessed valuation imply differences of more than $14,000 in annual tax liability. For a nonprofit organization operating at the very edge of its cash flow, an additional $14,000 in tax liability translates into a $5 a month rent increase (with HUD approval) or a serious cash deficit. The organization felt that with it now paying 18 percent of gross for property taxes, it had become nearly impossible to operate low-income housing.

Investor B in Portland was forced in place in escrow $28,000 to cover his annual property tax liability on a 236 project, since Portland maintains that it taxes these projects on "market value." As a precautionary measure, this investor estimated that he might be reassessed for 70-80 percent of FHA productions costs. To date, B has not been reassessed for any part of the $600,000 rehabilitation he carried out. Though thankful, B reports that if Portland does not intend to assess at close to construction costs, there are a series of 236 projects he would like to undertake. All that he requires is a clear understanding of his tax obligation.

The vulnerability of federally assisted projects to local tax policy can be seen from Table 6-1. Upward reassessment was much more likely to occur in federally subsidized rehabilitation or rehabilitation carried out by nonprofit sponsors than it was in private-market housing. Most municipalities seem to feel that tax increases in the former case are passed on to the federal government or the nonprofit sponsor and so represent a free good to the municipality. Unfortunately, in many instances this view is mistaken and higher marginal taxes resulting from upward reassessments are passed forward to the tenants in the form of higher rents.

From the point of view of investors, the present system for determining tax obligation on 236 projects has three defects. First of all, obtaining a property-tax commitment from the assessor often is the most time-consuming step in the application for a letter of feasibility. The operator of a 236 project in Chicago reported that "If a uniform rule existed for taxing 236 projects, we could speed up the application process by 45 days." This bureaucratic delay may ultimately discourage sponsors from participation in such programs. Second, the level of property taxation and the risk that assessment will be increased makes many 236 projects infeasible. So many risks exist in these programs that the additional risk of miscalculating a major cost such as property taxes can discourage investment altogether.[2] The state of Michigan now has legislation stipulating that nonprofit

Table 6-1
Reassessment of Private and Public Rehabilitation Projects

Expenditure Per Unit	Nonprofit and Government Aided Rehabilitation Projects		Private-Market Properties	
	No. of Projects	Percentage Reassessed	No. of Projects	Percentage Reassessed
Less than $500	1	0.0%	53	1.9%
$ 500 to $2,999	3	33.3	62	16.1
$ 3,000 to $9,999	7	57.1	30	13.3
$10,000 and over	5	100.0	7	57.1
Total	16	62.5	152	12.5

Sample: Residential structures built prior to 1961.
Notes: Federal government aided rehabilitation projects include 236, 221d3, and 312 loans and grants as part of a FACE program. (FACE is an acronym for federally-assisted code enforcement.) Other projects included in these categories are owned by nonprofit corporations set up to provide low or moderate income housing under various state regulations.

operators of 236 projects pay 10 percent of net shelter rent in lieu of property taxes.[3] One nonprofit organization in Detroit reported that, before passage of this legislation, it submitted to HUD a proposal for a 430 unit 236 project, which was rejected as infeasible. After passage of the legislation, the organization resubmitted its proposal. Its tax liability was now 33 percent less than the assessor's previous estimate, and the organization was guaranteed that this liability would not increase unless rental rates increased. The project was approved by HUD and how operates at 100 percent occupancy.

All operators of 236 projects agreed that a long queue of presently infeasible 236 projects would become feasible if taxes were fixed at a known low level of gross income. How greatly such a change in tax policy would affect overall investment depends, of course, on whether the present 236 program is constrained by a lack of feasible projects or a lack of budgetary funds. If the constraint is budgetary, the mere fact that more projects become feasible need not imply that more projects will be constructed.

Finally, once the development is constructed, 236 and 221(d)3 projects run the risk of having to absorb substantial tax increases due to changes in the basis for assessing properties. These must either be passed on to the tenant, raising the cost of housing to low-income families, or absorbed in the form of a reduced cash flow, increasing the probability that the operator will not be able to maintain mortgage payments after the exhaustion of depreciation benefits.

Smaller owners who had taken advantage of 3 percent rehabilitation loans under the 312 program reported that local tax policy consumed much of the subsidy of these programs. The owners believed, and Table 6-1 tends to confirm, that the assessor's office was much more active in reassessing 312 rehabilitation than it was in reassessing the same work where carried out privately. An effective 3 percent property tax levied on the cost of rehabilitation raises the interest and tax payment to 6 percent, comparable to what it would be on the private market without reassessment.

The Municipality's Perspective

From the point of view of the municipality, the objective in taxing 236 projects is to collect the maximum possible revenue without driving away the federally subsidized programs or making rent levels impossibly high for low-income families.[4]

Table 6-2 summarizes the tax formula presently used by each of the sample cities.

Those cities that tax 236 projects at a very low rate reported they feel they are doing so at the expense of their tax base. According to Baltimore's assessor, the agreement to tax 236 projects at 6 percent of gross rent was worked out by the city solicitor, against the judgment of the assessor's office. The assessor felt that the accumulation of tax-exempt low-income and elderly housing eventually would increase the tax burden on private-sector housing. He reported that already several private investors who had lost tenants to the subsidized projects had demanded that their assessment be reduced as well. Several other assessors reported that federally subsidized programs in their cities substituted for private investment. One effect of the program was to replace fully taxable properties with partially taxable property, reducing the city's tax base.

Table 6-2
Criteria for Assessing 236 Rehab Projects

City	Criteria
Atlanta	Now reviewing assessment standards, intend to increase assessments. Believe that subsidized projects should receive no tax concessions if they can generate positive cash flow when fully taxed.
Baltimore	6% of gross rent
Chicago	*Ad hoc* assessments—trying to work out standards with civic groups. "We need guidelines from the Feds."
Detroit	Nonprofit groups: 10% of net shelter rent; Profit groups: "Reasonable fraction" of construction cost.
Nashville	Unknown
Oklahoma City	236 Program just starting. No concessions.
Philadelphia	Now treat as if private rentals, assessment based on project's income; "awaiting additional information from federal authorities." Have several appeals pending.
Portland	Estimate sale value on private market.
Providence	12% of potential gross rent—5% vacancy allowance.
San Francisco	Use income approach, with adjustment for "lower quality" of income from 236 projects.

Those cities that tax 236 properties at a very high rate tend to see their actions as inducing a pure transfer of federal funds into municipal coffers. In Atlanta the assessors reported that HUD automatically permitted rent increases when a 236 project's tax liability increased, and that a substantial part of this rent increase was absorbed out of rent-supplement monies. Consequently, a significant proportion of local property taxes were absorbed directly by federal rent-supplement funds. The city seemed to follow a policy of taxing 236 programs at the maximum rate possible without discouraging their further construction.

Conclusion

As Table 6-2 makes clear, no agreement exists as to how 236 rehab projects should be taxed. This confusion extends to other federally subsidized developments like 221(d)3 projects and 312 rehabilitation loans. Several assessors requested federal guidelines on the subject.

Investors in 236 and 221(d)3 programs without exception preferred paying property taxes as a percentage of gross rents to paying a tax based on market value. They stressed that payment based on gross rent carried certainty regarding tax liability and the assurance that taxes would not increase unless rent levels increased. Without this certainty many private developers would choose not to build subsidized low-income housing.

In conclusion, assessors and investors alike felt that a simple, uniform standard was needed for the assessment of federally assisted housing. Investors currently involved in these projects noted that the difficulty of accurately forecasting property-tax burden seriously altered the effectiveness of these programs. Once these projects are completed, an unexpected change in property-tax assessment can damage the prospects for continuing successful operation.

With the high rate of default that already characterizes subsidized housing, resulting in vast problems of repossession for the federal government, it seems urgent to minimize the additional operating risk that comes from uncertainty regarding property-tax obligations.

7 Upward Transitional Neighborhoods

The potential disincentive effects of property taxation are greatest in the upward transitional neighborhoods, where property upgrading normally would be most vigorous. More than half the upward transitional properties in our sample had been rehabilitated with a median per unit expenditure of $2,300. In older cities where little space remains for new construction, this rejuvenation of the existing housing stock accounts for most of the increments in the cities' residential property base. Our sample revealed that city authorities are understandably reluctant to impose on upward transitional neighborhoods a tax burden that might destroy their growth or propel white residents out of the city into the suburbs.

The table of effective neighborhood tax rates (Table 3-3) shows that virtually all cities extended favorable tax treatment to upward transitional neighborhoods.

Property taxes may discourage neighborhood upgrading in two ways. The level of taxation may be so high that affluent whites, of the kind who are responsible for rediscovering "chic" downtown neighborhoods, prefer to reside outside the city. Dramatic restoration of aged and blighted housing stock is almost exclusively a white phenomenon, undertaken by families whose alternative residence is the suburbs. If the city's tax burden becomes too high or its service quality too low, the city is apt to lose these people and with them the housing investment they would have undertaken. Previous discussion indicated that most cities have gone to considerable lengths to keep the level of taxation in upward transitional neighborhoods from becoming burdensome.

The second potentially discouraging effect of property taxation is a marginal effect. If improvements to the housing stock are assessed for the incremental value they add to a property, the additional tax burden will lower the rate of return to such improvements and discourage investors from undertaking them. This marginal effect can occur at any overall level of taxation, though evidently the discouragement to investment will be most severe in those neighborhoods where incremental improvements are taxed at a high rate.

The Neighborhood

The typical upward transitional neighborhood from our sample was a well-defined geographic neighborhood composed of old, architecturally interesting housing stock. Often constructed as single-family homes, the structures over the

79

years had been converted to more intensive use and permitted to fall into disrepair. At some point, the neighborhood was rediscovered by young professionals and foresighted developers who valued access to downtown and recognized that by upgrading this old stock they could purchase high quality housing at much lower prices than was possible in new construction. The first entrants typically were small investors who intended to live in the neighborhood; not until neighborhood revival was well underway did large investors enter the area. As the quality of housing changed, so did the residents of the neighborhood. Young, white affluent professionals displaced older, poorer residents, many of whom were nonwhite. Four examples of the upward transitional neighborhood included in our sample were:

1. College Hill/Fox Point, Providence

College Hill contains a large number of eighteenth century merchants' homes, which up to 1956 served as slum tenements. In 1956 Brown University announced that it intended to demolish a large portion of the housing stock in order to construct a new dormitory. Reacting in opposition to this proposal, residents formed the Providence Preservation Society, which succeeded in having the neighborhood designated as historical site. One developer purchased sixteen buildings, then in crowded, multiunit use, and restored them as single-family homes; after a lag, others followed suit. Though all of the 400 homes of the original historical site were preserved, eventually the success of the College Hill restoration spread to fringe areas, like Fox Point, where rehabilitation of existing housing was combined with replacement of the worst portion of the stock by new multiunit structures. Aggressive "up-graders" in the Fox Point neighborhood have had the area approved for Section 312 loans and are exerting pressure on other owners to make use of the subsidized loans. At times this pressure has led to conflicts between the new residents, bent on rapid upgrading, and the Portuguese community, which sees the transformation of the housing stock as threatening its living patterns.

2. Lincoln Park, Chicago

In the nineteenth century, Lincoln Park was populated by beer barons and retail merchants. In later years, their lavish homes were converted to boarding houses or cheap multiunit rental stock. Lincoln Park became a point of entry for poor white migrants to Chicago. The revitalization of Lincoln Park occurred as a spillover from Old Town, a well publicized restoration project of the 1950s which, according to Lincoln Park residents, became overcommercialized. Some of the original residents of Old Town moved into Lincoln Park. One device they used to delimit the area was the deliberate exclusion of bars and package stores, which residents viewed as essential to upgrading the neighborhood. Of the upper transitional neighborhoods included in our study, Lincoln Park was one of the furthest along in development. Large-scale rehabilitation of the housing stock has been completed in many parts. Younger, wealthier residents have now moved into the neighborhood, giving it an artsy, swinging reputation. By now, much of the rehabilitation activity is in the hands of large-scale real-estate operators.

3. Couch, Portland

The housing stock in Portland is of more recent vintage than that of most other cities in our study. The predominant housing style in Couch is the wooden frame, single-family home, constructed between 1900 and 1930. Rehabilitation here is a more recent phenomenon than in Providence or Chicago, and, up to now, it has been carried out on a smaller scale. Several large homes, which had been converted to boarding houses, have now been converted back to single-family dwellings. Much minor repair and cosmetic rehabilitation have been carried out on other structures. No large realtors have entered the neighborhood. Investment has been delayed in part by fear that adverse zoning changes would destroy the residential character of the neighborhood. Adding to this uncertainty was the possibility that large sections of the area would undergo urban renewal in the form of an expansion of the Good Samaritan Hospital. In the judgment of residents both changes would destroy the residential character of the neighborhood. Property values have gone up greatly in the neighborhood as a result of the competition for land use, and the speculation against possible influences of urban renewal.

The neighborhoods described above are examples of private-market transition. Most cities also have transitional neighborhoods that were deliberately created by public policy. In order to contrast the styles of upgrading, we selected an urban renewal district as our upward transitional neighborhood in Detroit and a federally assisted code-enforcement area in San Francisco.

4. Buena Vista East, San Francisco

Until recently, this was a lower-middle-income neighborhood whose housing stock had been declining steadily as it aged. Dominated by small multiunit structures built between 1906-1930, the neighborhood possesses many amenities, easy access to downtown and structurally sound buildings. Yet, because the income of residents had not kept pace with escalating property taxes, maintenance and other operating costs, many structures accumulated minor code violations. Rejuvenation of the area was touched off when the city designated Buena Vista East as a concentrated code-enforcement area and made subsidized 3 percent loans and direct grants available. As upgrading spread, a number of young professionals purchased properties. To reinforce the neighborhood improvement stimulated by low-interest loans and technical assistance, the city made environmental improvements, including the repair of streets, curbs, and sidewalks and an increase in street lighting and tree planting. The gradual decline of the neighborhood has been reversed and property values have begun to increase.

The Market

Improvement of the housing stock plays a central role in investors' strategies in the upward transitional neighborhoods. Most investors in our sample bought their properties with the intention of expending substantial amounts in upgrading them, in return for which they expected to gain significant capital appreciation and (if owners of rental stock) to augment rental income significantly.

Respondents stressed that the profitability of investment in housing rehabilitation depends, above all, on the success of neighborhood upgrading. An investor can substantially rehab his own property, but if surrounding properties remain unimproved, the market will fail to value his investment even at cost. Conversely, in neighborhoods of active upgrading, individual properties will appreciate in value, even if no investment is made. Investors have adapted their strategy to these strong neighborhood effects.

Investor A in the College Hill section of Providence prefers to buy up two entire blocks of homes at a time. One block he rehabilitates in depth, at a cost of over $20,000 per unit, for professional families. The second block he rehabilitates just enough to replace the present, low-income tenants with students. The second block serves as a "buffer" for the first, putting some distance between the professional families and the blighted sections of the city. When the time is ripe, Investor A will further upgrade the second block of properties, and replace the students with professional families.

Investor B in Lincoln Park, Chicago, was one of several partners in a townhouse project. He recognized that, if successful, the project would upgrade substantially the tone of the immediate neighborhood. Accordingly, he acquired a nearby six-unit building, carried out external improvements and raised rents to reflect the better atmosphere of the block. This investor felt that "the only way to make sure that a neighborhood changes is to buy up enough properties to change it yourself."

By upgrading several properties at once, large investors can create "mini-neighborhoods" of their own. Smaller owners have to band together to achieve the same result. A prominent feature of each of the upward transitional neighborhoods studied was the strong neighborhood associations that existed. These neighborhood associations participated in whatever activity would boost the quality or reputation of the neighborhood.

The homeowners in Inman Park, Atlanta, meet once a week to exchange information about the neighborhood. Currently two issues are uppermost on their minds: the possibility of persuading banks to extend improvement loans to the neighborhood and the desire to discover ways to reduce costs of home improvement. To convince the banks that improvement loans in the neighborhood represent a good investment, leaders of the neighborhood association have invited bankers to their homes and conducted tours of the neighborhood—though to date without success. To compile information on home improvement techniques, residents pool their knowledge regularly as to where building materials can be purchased most cheaply and where skilled labor can be hired for restoration. Recently residents have attempted to capture some of the external benefits their own improvements have generated. One owner interviewed had acquired two adjacent houses. One he took as his personal residence and restored. The other he held in the conviction that the improvement in his own home, and the neighborhood, would make the adjacent property appreciate in value. This action imitates, on a small scale, the strategy of large investors who buy up entire blocks of property. At the time of interview, the neighborhood association was attempting to find ways in which it could, as a group, buy neighborhood properties, improve them, and offer them for resale at a profit.

Where neighborhood revival succeeds, the returns to capital investment in upward transitional neighborhoods can be very large. The median amount invested per housing unit in our sample was $2,300; the investor earned an average return, by way of capital appreciation and augmented rental income, that exceeded the rate of return on investment in all other neighborhoods.

While the payoffs are large, in the event that neighborhood upgrading succeeds, the investor runs the risk that his neighborhood will fail to take off. To be successful, the momentum of rehabilitation must increase from the outset. Otherwise, investors cannot hope to recover the expenditures made for improvements. Since typically the first entrants into the neighborhood are small investors, the availability of financing is a crucial concern, which respondents listed as the primary obstacle to neighborhood development. Banks are unwilling to extend improvement loans until it is clear that a neighborhood has turned the corner. Large investors, likewise, will not risk their capital until revival is well underway. The burden of risk-taking then falls on the small investor, who has the most difficult time gaining access to capital. Table 7-1 summarizes the sample information regarding the type of investor and investment found in the upward transitional neighborhoods.

The Role of Property Taxation

The potential impact of property taxes in upward transitional areas is very large. The possibility of large-scale investment in the housing stock exists in these neighborhoods, but the rate of return on such investments, and consequently, the probability of their taking place, is highly sensitive to tax policy. Some cities periodically reassess all properties in upward transitional neighborhoods on the grounds that capital appreciation is attributable principally to neighborhood improvement, not building-specific improvements. Other cities increase assessment only on those properties that have been upgraded. A taxation from serving as a disincentive to property or neighborhood improvement. Each of these tax strategies, which we now examine, has different implications for the housing stock.

Assessing Building-Specific Improvements

When a property is reassessed for the value of improvements made to it, a direct tax is placed on investments in the housing stock. If a city acts promptly in

Table 7-1
Distribution of Rehabilitation Activity by Size of Investor for Upward Transitional Neighborhoods

Size of Investor	Total Number of Properties	Percentage Rehabbing	Median Per Unit Expenditures on Rehabilitation	Percentage Maintaining or Upgrading Quality of Their Properties	Percentage Using Borrowed Funds
Single-family homeowners	8	75.0%	$4,000	87.5%	50.0%
Investors with:					
2 to 9 units	10	70.0	600	80.0	14.3
10 to 40 units	18	94.4	1,500	100.0	17.6
41 or more units	38	36.8	1,000	94.7	42.9
Total	74	59.5	2,300	93.2	29.5

Sample: Private-market residential structures built prior to 1961.

Notes: Percentage rehabbing gives proportion of the total number of properties in the relevant category with rehabilitation expenditures at any time in the period 1966 to 1970. Median Per Unit Expenditures on Rehabilitation have been rounded to the nearest $100. For further discussion of percentage maintaining or upgrading their properties, see Table 4-7.

Source: Investor Interview questions 3, 17a, and 21; and Homeowner Interview questions 6d, 14 and 18.

reassessing properties for the full value of improvements effected, the increased tax burden can cut sharply into the investor's rate of return. As an illustration, consider a $10,000 improvement which has a ten-year life for tax purposes, but which retains its economic value at the end of period. Suppose that by carrying out the investment, the owner can raise his rent roll by $1,700 annually and that 90 percent of the principal amount is financed by a 7.5 percent ten-year loan. We assume the property tax is set at 3 percent of market value. All of these figures are representative of the ones reported by respondents. Table 7-2 summarizes this typical investor's financial setup. It shows the rate of return the investor can earn if the city does not reassess his property, and the rate of return he can earn if the city assesses the improvement at its full cost. Building-specific reassessment in this instance reduces the investor's rate of return from 24.0 percent to 9.0 percent. Similar reductions in profitability would be enough in many cases to make an otherwise attractive housing investment unprofitable.

How is the practice of reassessing properties to reflect the value of improve-

Table 7-2
Impact of Reassessment Policy on Rate of Return to $10,000 Rehabilitation

Investor's Equity		Rate of Return with Reassessment $1000	Rate of Return No Reassessment $1000
Increased income per year		1700	1700
Average interest payment*		345	345
Depreciation (straight line)		1000	1000
Increased property tax		300	—
Profit for tax purposes =	(Income-Interest-Depreciation-Taxes)	55	355
Increased income tax (50%) bracket		28	178
Net income after taxes		27	177
Average principal payment*		937	937
Total cash flow =	(Net income + Depreciation- Principal Payments)	90	240
Cash flow as return on equity		9.0%	24.0%

*On a $9,000, 7 1/2%, 10 year loan ($9,000 is 90% of the improvement cost) the annual mortgage payment is $1,282. Over the 10 year period, the average annual interest payment is $345 and the average annual principal payment is $937.

ments? Most cities in our sample claimed to assess all improvements that increased a property's market value. Despite this, assessment practice varies substantially from one city to the next. Chicago calculates assessed valuations according to a formula which assigns values to buildings by age and structural type, while virtually ignoring any rehabilitation undertaken. The effect is to grant a *de facto* abatement for much investment in upgrading. One large investor in Lincoln Park reported that the Chicago assessor had assured him that if he rehabilitated structures built prior to 1870, he would not be reassessed no matter how much he expended on improvement. Investors in Oklahoma City reported that the only improvements resulting in reassessment were those which increased the floor space of a dwelling unit. Even in cities professing to assess every improvement, exceptions seemed to be made in the case of upward transitional neighborhoods. Baltimore, for instance, has a policy of assessing improvements, but the very substantial improvements made in Bolton Hill have, for the most part, gone unassessed. As elsewhere, the explanation seems to lie in the assessor's unwillingness to nip in the bud neighborhood revitalization by levying a tax on it.

Assessing Neighborhoods for Increases
in Market Value

Neighborhood reassessment assesses entire geographical areas to reflect the changing market values of properties. The extent of neighborhood reassessment varied greatly among our sample cities. Detroit reassesses every neighborhood in

Table 7-3
Reassessment of Rehabilitation in Upward Transitional Neighborhoods

Rehabilitation Expenditures	Number of Properties with Rehabilitation Expenditures	No. of Properties Reassessed as a Result of Rehabilitation	Percentage Reassessed
$ 0 to $ 499	13	1	7.7%
$ 500 to $2,999	13	4	30.8
$ 3,000 to $9,999	15	3	20.0
$10,000 +	6	4	66.7
All Properties	47	12	25.5

Sample: Private-market residential structures built prior to 1961 with any rehabilitation expenditures in the period 1966-1970.

Notes: See Table 3-10 and 3-11 for comparison of reassessment by neighborhoods.

Source: Investor Interview questions 17a, and 20a; Homeowner Interview question 14, 17, and Property Data Sheet question 4.

the city on the basis of the previous year's assessment/sales ratio. Oklahoma City has not had a neighborhood reassessment since 1952. The remaining cities fall between these extremes, with neighborhood reassessments carried out at intervals of different lengths. Chicago attempts to reassess neighborhoods every four years; Baltimore has a neighborhood schedule which calls for reassessment every five years.

Like building-specific taxation, neighborhood reassessment on balance increases the tax burden of investors in upward transitional neighborhoods because property values, by definition, are increasing in these neighborhoods. However, the marginal effects on the housing stock of the two measures is quite different. If the entire neighborhood is reassessed, no special burden is borne by the investor who upgrades his property. There is no marginal disincentive to investment in the housing stock. In fact, reassessing properties by neighborhood is a form of land-value taxation, since the distinguishing feature of a neighborhood is the location of its residential land. In theory, neighborhood assessment should tax properties according to the optimal use for land in that neighborhood. Since in the case of upward transitional neighborhoods, the optimal land use involves upgrading (or replacing) the existing housing stock, neighborhood assessment ought to encourage housing investment. This is just the reverse of the marginal effect of imposing a tax on building-specific improvements.

That is the theory. However, several respondents reported that in practice neighborhood taxation can also discourage upgrading. Large investors feared that reassessing neighborhoods on the basis of a few sales of upgraded properties would make it impossible for commercial rehabbers to operate in the area. These firms typically buy up a number of properties at one time. Some of the properties they rehabilitate immediately; others they hold until neighborhood revival generates more demand. If all properties in the neighborhood are reassessed on the basis of the first sales, the cost of carrying unimproved properties for future rehabilitation becomes prohibitive. Planned phasing of rehabilitation then becomes impossible, with the risk that neighborhood revitalization never will get off the ground.

Long-time residents of neighborhoods where land prices recently have begun to increase feel that assessing the land at the new, higher value is especially prejudicial to them. Although their income stream has not increased, these families are obliged to pay higher taxes. Many feel that the city's assessment policy is driving them from their homes.

Neighborhood assessment undoubtedly imposes some burden on long-time residents and, if pushed too soon, may shut off some neighborhood upgrading, but its discincentive to investment in upward transitional neighborhoods is minimal. In fact, applied prudently, it should provide a positive incentive to investment. Since, as we have argued in previous chapters, neighborhood assessment has highly beneficial consequences for the poorer sections of the city, it seems a desirable policy to encourage.

Abatements

Assessors in several cities reported that, in their judgment, there are two factors in elastic supply to the cities that can be affected by assessment policy. One factor is the supply of capital to the housing market. The second factor is white, middle-class population. Special concessions have been made to retain both factors. In addition to the *de facto* abatements on housing improvements granted in Chicago and Oklahoma City as well as in certain neighborhoods in other cities, Providence has adopted an explicit abatement policy, which promises investors five years' freedom from reassessment on improvements. Just as these measures are designed to keep capital invested in the city, so other concessions seem to have been made to retain white middle-class families in the city. Though no assessor admitted to deliberately underassessing upward transitional neighborhoods in order to keep professional whites in the city, many expressed their fears that if assessments became too high in these neighborhoods, the white population would desert the city. Among other undesirable consequences, this exodus would slow down drastically the upgrading of the residential housing stock in transitional neighborhoods.

Conclusion

Concern about the effects of property taxation often focuses on the deterrent the tax is supposed to provide to neighborhood upgrading. Our analysis suggests that this concern has been exaggerated. At present, relatively few housing improvements are reassessed. Overall, the level of property taxation in upward transitional neighborhoods is lower than that found in other neighborhoods. This was especially true of the upward transitional neighborhoods in Baltimore, Chicago, Philadelphia, and Providence. All evidence indicates that the poorer neighborhoods of many cities are being forced to subsidize heavily, through tax payments, the special tax concessions granted to residents of upward transitional neighborhoods where revitalization is strongest, capital appreciation most likely, and residents most affluent.

We have no desire to minimize the importance of neighborhood rejuvenation nor underestimate its effect on the spirit of a city. However, the potential capital gains to investment in upward transitional areas are very large. No additional tax subsidy is required to provide attractive investment opportunities. As reported by investors, the primary obstacle to the neighborhood upgrading is the unavailability of financing for property improvement, especially at the early stage of neighborhood revitalization. Tax concessions represent a considerable income transfer to the wealthy residents of stable and upward transitional neighborhoods; but they are an inefficient way to encourage housing investment, which is better achieved by direct subsidy or improvement loans.

8 Stable Neighborhoods

Over the short run, the housing market in stable neighborhoods is less affected by the property tax than housing markets in other parts of the city. For instance, two-thirds of the operators of rental stock in stable neighborhoods reported that they were able to pass on to tenants the full amount of any increase in property taxes. This figure contrasts with 45 percent of the owners in downward transitional areas and only 24 percent in blighted areas who felt that they were able to increase rents enough to offset property-tax increases. Under conditions where the property-tax burden is fully shifted to the tenant, the real-estate operator acts as little more than tax collector for the local government. Over the long run, of course, the higher price that tenants have to pay for rental housing will have some effect on the demand for housing, but over the short run landlords are least likely to feel the impact of the property tax when they can pass the tax burden on in the form of higher rents.

In a longer perspective, operators of rental stock in the older cities almost to a man expressed the fear that suburban competition threatened the future stability of their cities' upper- and middle-class neighborhoods. While the social ills associated with the core city—like its crime rate and deteriorating schools—invade downtown middle-class neighborhoods before they reach the suburbs, the capacity of the city to combat these trends through increased public expenditures seems to be declining, relative to the fiscal capacity of the suburbs. The result is a vicious spiral, wherein the press of urban problems forces some well-to-do families and businesses to escape to the suburbs, taking their contribution to the tax base with them, while the resultant loss of tax revenue incapacitates the city government in its efforts to cope with these problems through the provision of better-quality public services. In city after city, government officials spoke of the urgency of not letting tax policy convert the central city into a repository for the poor.

Like the housing problem of blighted neighborhoods, however, the city's fiscal and public-service problems, which are of foremost concern to many investors in stable neighborhoods, prove difficult to fit under a single description. One common diagnosis holds that the urban fiscal crisis has its cause in the cities' inferior property-tax base. If this is so, the remedy would seem to follow at once. There must be tax-base equalization, either at the metropolitan level or across the state as a whole. The legal profession has been particularly active in agitating for conversion to a tax method, sometimes called power equalization, which would guarantee that equal property-tax rates would raise equal amounts of tax revenue per household, whatever the property wealth of a particular jurisdiction. In effect, these proposals would have local jurisdictions apply their property-tax rates to the average level of property wealth in the state as a whole rather than to local wealth alone, as is presently the case.

Proposals such as these confront decision-makers with an unhappy dilemma. While property-tax-base equalization would immensely improve the competitiveness of some central cities, for others it would represent a financial disaster by destroying the one advantage that most central cities now possess: a concentration of taxable commercial and industrial property, which makes it possible for the cities to raise a dollar of tax revenue at a lower tax rate than is possible for most other jurisdictions.

The Neighborhood

The terms in which the residents of stable neighborhoods perceive suburban alternatives can best be conveyed by example:

Palmer Park, Detroit

Palmer Park is a residential district at the extreme north of the city of Detroit. Although city officials agreed it was Detroit's closest approximation to a stable rental market, vacancy rates have begun to creep up and several area owners who were interviewed believed that the area already has begun to decline. For some, "decline" is a matter of racial transition. For others, "decline" is a matter of deteriorating neighborhood appearance and poor-quality public services. Several residents emphasized that Palmer Park, the large park which gave the area its name, no longer could be used safely. The decline in school quality is even more pronounced. The proportion of families sending their children to public schools has declined drastically in Palmer Park. In fact, the white population left in this neighborhood and in Detroit as a whole is an aging population, composed largely of families that do not have school-aged children and do not have the mobility that would make a move to the suburbs easy to carry out. The median age of the city's white population now is thirty-six, far above the national average. In several of the buildings we examined, the average age of residents was in excess of sixty.

Guilford, Baltimore

The neighborhood of Guilford in Baltimore is an area of older single-family homes, originally developed for wealthy families. Unlike Palmer Park—a rental district which has an aging population—the attractive single-family homes in Guilford have been purchased in large part by young professionals. Most of the homeowners interviewed said that by purchasing a home in Guilford they had made a deliberate decision to stay in the city rather than move to the suburbs. In each case, respondents reported that the majority of their colleagues at work lived in the suburbs. They displayed a keen awareness of the relative tax rates in Baltimore City and Baltimore County. Several stated that if by the time their children grew to school-age, they could not enroll them in the local public schools, they, too, would be obliged to move to the suburbs. The impression conveyed was that there were enough young professional families with a preference for city life to sustain demand for the few affluent neighborhoods in Baltimore City, but that if the cost of city living increased by very much, these families would join the flight to the suburbs.

While this sharp contrast between suburb and city typified the response of residents in the older and larger cities, elsewhere the distinction was muted or even reversed. A large builder-developer in the Atlanta area judged that, on balance, the higher tax rate in the city was justified by the superior public services provided there. For instance, the housing he built within Atlanta's Fire Protection Zone qualified for lower insurance premiums.

The Housing Market and the Property Tax

Tax and public-service competition between the suburbs and central city has received a great deal of attention in the professional economic literature.[1] There seems to be agreement that in this competition the central city is at a severe disadvantage in terms of its tax base. However, the precise terms of the city's handicap usually is left unclear. Most often it is implied that the city's present tax base lags far behind the suburban tax base. At other times, attention focuses on the slow rate of growth of the city's taxable property.

To shed some light on the nature of city-suburban fiscal competition and the extent to which property-tax reform can alleviate it, we have examined in detail data for two of our sample cities—Detroit and Baltimore. Both of these cities are usually considered to be classic victims of the urban crisis. Both have crime rates that rank among the top five in the nation. Both have faced severe financial crises. The continuing threat that Detroit will have to terminate its school year in midseason because of the repeated failure of local citizens to authorize higher school taxes has attracted national attention. In fact, in only one important respect do the two metropolitan areas obviously differ from each other. While Detroit is surrounded by a large number of fragmented suburban jurisdictions, each with its own taxing powers (and even has two separate jurisdictions—Hamtramck and Highland Park—which lie entirely within its boundaries), the only taxing powers in the Baltimore area are the city of Baltimore on the one hand and Baltimore County, which encompasses the entire suburban area.

Baltimore City

Baltimore City displays in exaggerated form all the fiscal difficulties that conventionally are identified with older cities. In terms of residential property values, Baltimore City's total tax base of $2,650 per capita compares with a per capita value of $4,490 in the rest of the metropolitan area.[2] This 70 percent difference in residential taxable wealth, of course, simply reflects the fact that suburban residents by and large earn greater incomes and can afford higher-value residential housing. This greater level of average residential wealth means that any given amount of tax revenue per household can be raised at a lower tax rate in the suburbs than in the city. Moreover, the city's disadvantage is compounded by an additional discrepancy in the value of industrial and commercial property. In 1970 the per capita value of such property was $3,920 in the suburbs, but only $3,070 in the city. This latter comparison is quite extraordinary, for it indicates that despite the central city's reputation as the industrial and commercial center of the metropolitan area, it lags behind the suburbs by almost 25 percent in the per capita value of nonresidential property. The suburbs' emergence as the principal employment center during the 1960s promises to continue to erode the relative fiscal capacity of Baltimore City in the future.

In the face of this markedly lower ability to raise tax revenue from its property base, the city of Baltimore has been called upon to maintain sharply higher public-service expenditure levels than have the suburbs. Per capita expenditures on some key items in the local budget are summarized in Table 8-1. What stands out from this table is that expenditures on three services—public safety, health and hospitals, and public welfare—account for the bulk of the extra spending obligations borne by the city. A similar pattern holds true in most other metropolitan areas.[3] Note that per capita expenditure on public schools is almost identical in the city and suburb (although the reputation of Baltimore City's school system is decidedly inferior).

The gap between Baltimore City's tax base and expenditure requirements has been met in part by state aid, which now assumes a substantial portion of the city's welfare bill and underwrites a considerable portion of the city's school expenditures. However, much of the revenue gap has had to be filled by a higher rate of property taxation in the city than in the suburbs. It is estimated that in 1970 Baltimore City's true property tax rate, as a proportion of market value, came to 2.8 percent compared to 1.5 percent in the suburbs. On a $40,000 house the tax differential between city and suburban living would then amount to more than $500 a year, in return for which residents of the city's affluent neighborhoods would not seem to receive any public-service advantage. It is natural, then, that city governments should try to compensate for the suburbs' edge by granting special treatment to their higher-income residents. Several assessors conceded that they were reluctant to impose full tax burdens on higher income residential property because they knew that the consequence would be to drive households into the suburbs. This may explain a good share of the neighborhood variation in assessment rates reported in Chapter 3.

Detroit

While the experience of Baltimore tends to confirm the usual view that the cities stand at a disadvantage in terms of their present property-tax base, the

Table 8-1

City and Suburb Tax and Expenditure Levels: Baltimore SMSA, 1970-1971

	City	Suburbs
1. Total local taxes per capita	$214.30	$194.30
2. Property taxes per capita	162.30	126.00
3. Effective property tax rate	2.8%	1.5%
4. Public safety expenditures, per capita	99.80	27.10
5. Public welfare expenditures, per capita	98.50	11.90
6. Health and hospitals expenditures per capita	42.20	6.60
7. School expenditure per capita	169.20	168.10
8. Total current expenditures per capita	579.70	272.30

Source: William H. Oakland, "Financing Urban Government: The Case of Baltimore," paper delivered at the Committee for Urban Economy Conference, January 12-13, 1973.

experience of Detroit suggests that this is far from universally true. On the surface, Detroit's financial problems would, if anything, seem even more severe than Baltimore's. In addition to the continuing school-finance crisis in Detroit, the city of Hamtramck, which is appropriately considered part of the core city since it lies entirely within the bounds of Detroit, has (according to the Advisory Commission on Intergovernmental Relations) come the closest to bankruptcy of any United States community since the depression. The Michigan State government has had to intervene in Hamtramck to guarantee the timely repayment of the city's debt.

Upon closer inspection, however, it turns out that whatever the source of Detroit's and Hamtramck's fiscal difficulties, it is not an inadequate property base. Table 8-2 compares the property-tax base and property-tax rates of selected low-, middle-, and high-income areas of the Detroit metropolitan region. As can be seen, Detroit's property-tax base exceeds that of most the middle-income suburbs with which it competes. In fact, it is the low-income "suburbs" of the area that have the highest per pupil property-tax bases. These areas contain the bulk of the region's industrial and commercial property, which gives local citizens a powerful edge when it comes to buying public services.

The plain fact of the matter is that Detroit faces a school-finance crisis for the simple reason that the city's school-tax rates are much lower than average for the metropolitan area. To some extent, the refusal to vote higher school taxes is the

Table 8-2

City and Suburban Income, Tax and Expenditure Levels: Detroit SMSA, 1970-1971

Jurisdiction	Median Family Income[1]	Per Pupil Property Tax Base 1970-71[2]	School Tax Rate 1970-71[3]	Other City and County County Property Taxes 1970[3]	Expenditures Per Pupil in Public Schools 1970-71[2]
Detroit	$10,045	$37,000	1.2%	1.7%	$ 920
High-Income Suburbs					
Bloomfield Hills	46,715	56,000	2.1	1.4	1,200
Birmingham	17,292	55,000	1.9	1.2	1,120
Grosse Point	19,020	61,000	1.6	1.4	1,200
Farmington	16,819	36,000	2.0	0.7	920
Southfield	18,141	63,000	1.7	0.7	1,040
Middle-Income Suburbs					
East Detroit	12,943	25,000	2.0	1.1	860
Ferndale	11,525	35,000	1.9	1.4	930
Hazel Park	11,208	29,000	1.9	1.3	900
Inkster	11,290	16,300	1.7	1.4	880
Lincoln Park	12,131	31,000	1.4	1.1	820
Roseville	12,262	24,000	1.8	1.1	820
Low-Income Suburbs					
Ecorse	9,706	89,000	1.0	1.5	1,010
Hantramck	9,395	81,000	1.2	1.5	1,200
Highland Park	8,716	49,000	2.0	1.4	1,200
River Rouge	9,433	120,000	1.1	1.4	1,390

Sources:

[1] U.S. Census, *Census of Social and Economic Characteristics*, 1970.

[2] *Ranking of Michigan Public School Districts by Selected Financial Data, 1970-1971.* Bulletin 1012, Michigan Department of Education, 1971.

[3] Michigan State Tax Commission, *1971 City and Village Tax Levy.*

result of selective migration. The white families who place high value on schooling for the most part already have left Detroit for the suburbs. Those who remain in the city are largely older families, with no personal stake in school expenditures and little inclination to pay higher school taxes for the benefit of black households who still are a minority of the city's population.

Conclusion

The point we wish to emphasize in this chapter is that the residents of the cities' stable neighborhoods almost always have in mind a suburban alternative to their present location. In most older metropolitan areas the suburbs enjoy a distinct advantage over the central city in terms of the quality of important public services like public schooling or crime protection. When a tax advantage is added to this service-quality advantage, the fiscal attraction of suburban residential sites is obvious.

One policy measure that often has been advocated to correct this fiscal imbalance is tax-base equalization. However, in this chapter we have seen that for Detroit and many other industrial cities, tax-base equalization would provide no cure at all for the urban fiscal crisis. Indeed, it is difficult to perceive how inner-city jurisdictions like Hamtramck and Highland Park could survive a sudden move to tax-base equalization. Whereas in Baltimore the financial crisis of the city is correctly seen as a consequence of tax-base inadequacy, in Detroit it has been precipitated by mounting expenditure requirements coupled with taxpayer unwillingness to pay for these expenditures despite possession of above-average tax bases.

Implementing the
Property-Tax System

Previous chapters on the neighborhood submarkets have demonstrated that the consistency of assessment/sales estimation varies greatly by city. This chapter considers the institutional reasons that make some assessment systems function better than others. Assessment methods, appeal procedures, reassessment practices, and other administrative features of the property-tax system are evaluated for their impact on assessment efficiency.

Dispersion of Assessment/Sales Ratios

The usual criterion for judging the effectiveness of a city's assessment procedures is the dispersion of its assessment/sales ratios. The first column of Table 9-1 presents data for 1966 from the Census of Governments, ranking the ten sample cities in order of increasing dispersion of assessment/sales ratios for single-family homes. For a city to have a low dispersion measure signifies that when properties in different locations come on the market, they sell at approximately the same multiple of their assessed valuation.

The coefficient of dispersion is a measure of random error. It is a valid measure of assessment performance only if deviations in the assessment/sales ratio are, in fact, randomly distributed. From the point of view of public policy, it is more important to determine whether there is a systematic variation in assessment/sales ratios; whether, that is, certain neighborhoods or types of property are discriminated against in the assessment procedure. A city with a low coefficient of dispersion may be assessing its properties more equitably than a city with a high dispersion number, if in the former case all properties share an equal probability of being under- or overassessed, whereas in the latter case properties in poor neighborhoods are systematically overassessed and properties in affluent neighborhoods systematically underassessed.

A good measure of systematic dispersion is provided by the neighborhood breakdown of our sample. The second column of Table 9-1 presents values of

$$Q = \frac{\text{Assessment/Sales Ratio in Blighted Neighborhood}}{\text{Assessment/Sales Ratio in Upward Transitional Neighborhood}}$$

A value of Q in excess of 1.0 indicates that properties in blighted neighborhoods bear a greater tax burden than properties in upward transitional neighborhoods. A value of Q below 1.0 indicates that blighted neighborhoods bear a lesser burden.

97

Table 9-1
Dispersion of Assessment/Sales Ratios by City

City	Coefficient of Dispersion,[a] 1966	Systematic Variation Q,[b] 1970
Providence	15.4	5.2
Portland	18.3	.8
Atlanta	18.3	2.2
Oklahoma City	18.7	1.1
Nashville	19.0	.8
Detroit	20.4	1.2
Baltimore	24.3	11.5
Chicago	24.5	13.2
Philadelphia	26.3	10.3
San Francisco	28.9	1.0

[a]Standard deviation about median.

$$ {}^{b}Q = \frac{\text{Assessment/Sales Ratio in Blighted Neighborhood}}{\text{Assessment/Sales Ratio in Upward Transitional Neighborhood}} $$

Notes: Standard deviation about median is a measure of dispersion about a central value, the median. It is the sum of the squared difference between the sample median and the individual observations. The figures for 1966 are based on all single-family homes for which assessment and sales information was collected by the Census of Governments. Comparison of the two columns should be guarded because of the vastly different sample sizes involved.

Source: U.S. Bureau of Census, Census of Governments, 1967, *Property Taxes*, and Investor Interview question 8, Homeowner Interview question 7, and Property Data Sheet question 4.

By and large, the two columns of Table 9-1 show only slight agreement between the ranking of cities by random and systematic dispersion measures. Most interesting are two cities, Detroit and San Francisco, which rank badly on the former scale but well on the latter. Both of these cities have reformed their assessment systems drastically since 1966, with the explicit intention of reducing the dispersion in assessment/sales ratio. The great improvement they register in the second column of Table 9-1 probably reflects the achievements of their reforms more than any contradiction between the two measures of dispersion. Providence's excellent score in column 1 is partly explained by the fact that the city has a total of only 15,000 single-family homes, almost all of which are clustered in the better-off sections of the city.

Assessment Methods

Professional appraising recognizes three basic approaches to estimating the "true cash value" of a residential rental property. Sales of comparable properties may be taken as a direct indication of market price. Capitalization of the property's income stream may be used to estimate market price. Or the true cash value may be estimated as reproduction costs corrected for depreciation. If a well-functioning market exists, the first two approaches should yield the same value, since the market value of a property "is" the net present value of its income stream, corrected for risk. Estimating true cash value as reproduction costs corrected for depreciation, however, is likely to yield a figure seriously at variance with the other two. This approach recognizes supply costs only. It ignores demand conditions, which may cause a property of a certain type in a certain location to be worth far more (or less) than the cost of replacement.

In addition to these three basic approaches for assessing properties, several cities in our sample made use of the gross-rent multiplier approach. The gross-rent multiplier is the market value of a property divided by its annual gross-rental receipts. Where variable gross-rent multipliers are used, these may provide a reliable rule of thumb as to market value. For instance, new luxury apartments may be valued at seven times gross rents and old blighted properties at two times, because these are the gross-rent multipliers that market prices in fact imply. Where a uniform gross-rent multiplier for all properties is applied, however, this method of assessment converts a tax on capital into a sales tax, which is much more regressive. If the market's gross-rent multipliers for luxury and blighted properties are seven and two respectively, but the assessor's office applies a uniform multiplier of five, then luxury buildings must be underassessed and blighted buildings overassessed. In order to ensure that this does not happen, however, the assessor must determine what is the appropriate gross-rent multiplier for a variety of different structure types and neighborhood conditions. This of course requires the application of one of the appraisal techniques discussed above such as the review of sales of comparable properties.

Whichever approach a city uses to assess properties in the first instance, it can maintain a check on the accuracy of its assessments by calculating assessment/sales ratios for diverse neighborhoods in the city. The evidence of the survey indicates that adjusting assessed valuations for all properties in a given neighborhood on the basis of observed deviations of assessment/sales ratios from the target level is the most cost-effective means of reducing dispersion.

Table 9-2 summarizes the criteria the several cities use in assessing properties and the interval at which they carry out reassessment.

The cities maintaining the lowest dispersion measures are those which give the most importance to market value in making assessments. The assessment systems in Portland and San Francisco, for instance, have the sole objective of duplicating market value. In both cases, state legislation empowers the state government to withhold certain transfers to the cities in the event that assessment/sales ratios deviate too much from the state-wide target. In fact, the Department of Revenue in Oregon has the power "to order any county board of equalization or county assessor to adjust the valuation of a property or class of property deemed necessary so that all taxable property is equalized between

Table 9-2
Assessment Standards by City

City	Assessment Formulas	Neighborhood Cycle	Use of Neighborhood Assessment/Sales Ratios to Confirm Assessments
Atlanta	• Gross-rent multiplier also other criteria	No general cycle Reassess neighborhoods with greatest sales activity	No
Baltimore	• Homes: comparable sales • Industrial: reproduction costs • Rental: variable rent properties • Multiplier	5 years	Yes
Chicago	• Replacement-depreciation	4 years	No
Detroit	• Replacement-depreciation • Comparables • Capitalized income stream	No general cycle Reassess all neighborhoods where assessment/sales ratios out of line	Yes

Nashville	• Capitalize standard income formula by building type	No general cycle Reassess neighborhoods with greatest sales activity	No
Oklahoma City	• Use classification formula giving cost per sq. ft. of new construction and rate of depreciation by property type	No general cycle Last city-wide reassessment in 1952	No
Philadelphia	• No set formula	No general cycle	No
Portland	• Cost-depreciation neighborhood adjustment • Comparable sales • Capitalized income stream	5 years	Yes
Providence	• Replacement cost-depreciation • Capitalized income stream • Comparable sales	No general cycle Last city-wide reassessment in 1960	No
San Francisco	• Comparable sales • Replacement cost-depreciation	No general cycle Reassess all neighborhoods where assessment/sales ratios more than 6% off target	Yes

Source: Assessor Interview.

taxpayers, between counties, and between taxing units to the end that equality of taxation according to law shall be secured." In both Oregon and California, as well as other states, the state government audits the performance of local assessment offices by conducting an independent assessment/sales ratio at designated intervals. Through close supervision and computerized record keeping random checks are made on the accuracy of sales ratios. As indicated in Table 9-1 the supervision of property-tax administration by these two states has been very successful.

The most manifestly professional assessment operation was that of Portland, Oregon. Portland maintains a complete computer file on every property in the city, which is open to all citizens. Properties are reassessed on a five-year cycle. When an inspector goes to a project, he carries with him the record of building permits that have been filed for that property. Properties are reassessed for both the specific improvements which have been carried out and for the overall changes in neighborhood values which have occurred since the last assessment. To reduce the magnitude of reassessment, at five-year intervals, the assessor recently adopted the practice of increasing the assessed valuation of all properties, not specifically being reassessed, by 4 percent annually. Portland goes further toward land-value taxation than any other city in the sample. If a land parcel is not in its optimal use, it is assessed at the market value it would have in optimal use minus the costs of converting it to that use. This means that improvements on some properties carry a negative assessment since their presence only adds to the cost of converting to optimal use.

Chicago, on the contrary, pays no attention to market value in its original assessment. The city follows a four-year neighborhood assessment cycle, but assessed valuations are determined on the basis of a structure's reproduction costs and depreciation. No attempt is made to make reassessments reflect changes in neighborhood property values or the income-generating possibilities of a structure, unless the assessment is appealed. At the time of appeal, market value and net income are admitted as grounds for revising the assessed valuation. But the responsibility for introducing market considerations into the assessment procedure lies entirely with the owner. It is obvious that in upward transitional neighborhoods, properties will be grossly underassessed, since the depreciation formula recognizes that these structures are very old, while ignoring the fact that property values are rapidly appreciating. In blighted neighborhoods, properties will be vastly overassessed, since the assessment formula pays no attention to the depressing effect neighborhood conditions have on market value.

Assessing Improvements

Previous chapters have established that most improvements do not, in fact, result in reassessment. This is especially true for nongovernment aided rehabilitation where only 12.5 percent of the units rehabilitated were actually reassessed. Obviously, local assessors do not want to discourage private reconstruction efforts. In fact, in most central cities in our sample even improvements to commercial properties were seldom reassessed, although the frequency was higher than for residential properties. Nevertheless, investor misunderstanding over reassessment persists. In most cities tremendous confusion reigns as to reassessment policy. Again and again, investors reported that they thought they would be reassessed for improvements which, according to the assessor's office, never lead to reassessment. In several instances, investors reported that they had been reassessed as a result of their rehabilitation activity when, in fact, assessor's records revealed that no reassessment had occurred. (See Table 9-3.)

Table 9-4 illustrates this discrepancy between investor's perceptions and assessor's practice for residential property owners. In no city did the assessor admit to reassessment of all exterior improvements. Indeed our sample indicates that only the largest of rehabilitation jobs are reassessed. Despite this fact, one-third of all investors interviewed felt that any exterior improvement they carried out would result in reassessment.

Among our sample cities, San Francisco has devised what seems to be the most efficient remedy for the confusion regarding which improvements result in reassessment. The assessor's office publishes a slim pamphlet listing a large number of frequently made improvements which the city does not reassess. Any

Table 9-3
Rehabilitation of Commercial Properties

	Number of Properties	Percentage of Properties
Total commercial properties	30	100%
With rehabilitation expenditures	12	40
Reassessed as result of rehabilitation	3	10

Sample: All commercial property investors responding to the questioning.
Source: Investor Interview.

Table 9-4
Investors Expectations of Reassessment of Exterior Improvements by City (Percentage of All Investors Who Felt That Any Exterior Improvement Would Lead to Reassessment)

	Number Responding	Percentage "Yes"		Number Responding	Percentage "Yes"
Atlanta	17	35.3%	Oklahoma City	14	42.9%
Baltimore	13	61.5	Philadelphia	15	26.7
Chicago	15	60.0	Portland	23	17.4
Detroit	16	45.5	San Francisco	12	33.3
Nashville	21	9.6	Total	146	32.2

Sample: All investors responding to the questioning.
Source: Investor Interview question 19b.

investor can inquire at the office beforehand to determine if a proposed improvement will be reassessed or not. Detroit has recently initiated a similar program.

A clear statement of reassessment policy is required in all cities. One of the ironies of the present system is that assessors themselves tend to exaggerate the amount of reassessment that occurs on building-specific improvements. Because the law requires them to assess all increases in market value, assessors are reluctant to admit that, in fact, many improvements are not assessed. Whatever disincentive the property tax provides for building improvements is more a result of investors' misconceptions as to assessment practice than of the actual practice.

Costs of Operation

The most efficient assessment system, from the point of view of performance, need not be the most cost-effective if the cost of operating it is extremely high. As shown in Table 9-5, Portland's system, which undoubtedly was the most professional, also has by far the highest per property cost of operation. Portland's assessment budget exceeds that of Philadelphia, which contains almost three times as many properties and five times as many people. However, with the exception of Portland there is only a weak correlation between per property costs of operation and performance levels, as measured in Tables 9-1 and 9-5.

The most cost-effective means of reducing the dispersion of assessment/sales ratios seems to be a continued checking of neighborhood ratios, followed by

Table 9-5
Costs of Assessment Systems by City

City	Separately Listed Parcels	1971 Assessor's Budget	Cost per Parcel	Cost per Capita
Atlanta	180,000	$ 840,000	$ 4.52	$1.91
Baltimore	250,000	700,000	2.80	0.77
Chicago	1,300,000	5,000,000	3.85	1.49
Detroit	423,000	1,800,000	4.26	1.08
Nashville	136,000	350,000	2.58	0.78
Oklahoma City	220,000	375,000	1.70	1.02
Philadelphia	550,000	2,500,000	4.55	1.28
Portland	200,000	3,000,000	15.00	7.83
Providence	45,000	196,000	4.36	1.09
San Francisco	154,000	2,020,000	13.12	2.82

Source: Assessor Interview.

neighborhood-wide reassessment whenever a neighborhood ratio gets out of line with the target level. This is the method used by Detroit, Portland, and San Francisco. The expense of Portland's system lies in its detailed visual inspection of each property. In Detroit, where visual inspection is much less common, the costs of operation are also much lower.

Detroit offers a good example of an assessment system which operates efficiently, yet inexpensively. Beginning in 1967, the assessor's office divided the city into 613 neighborhoods. Records are kept of all sales, and median assessment/sales ratios are calculated annually for each neighborhood. If in a given year a neighborhood ratio exceeds the 50 percent level stipulated by law, assessments in the next year are lowered in that neighborhood. If the assessment/sales ratio falls below 50 percent, assessments are raised. In four years of operation Detroit's system has significantly reduced the neighborhood spread in assessment/sales ratios.

Use of Computers

One of the most cost-effective and efficient methods for mass property appraisals is through the use of computers.[1] By applying multiple-regression techniques, the independent contribution of each component of property (interior space, age of building, neighborhood, number of rooms, etc.) to the total price can be calculated. Once the contribution of each individual factor is determined, the market value of other properties can be predicted by multiplying the dollar value of each component (e.g., each square foot of floor space adds $5.00 to the market value) by the amount of that component present (e.g., 1500 square feet of floor space are "worth" $7500 in market value). Using the computer to estimate market values is similar, in principle, to the appraisers use of market-data spread sheets. The advantage of the computer, however, is that its statistical estimates are less impressionistic because a price index can be calculated for a massive number of properties in a much shorter time.

Appeals Procedure

In a system where assessments are erratically determined or systematically biased, the possibility of remedy through the appeals procedure is extremely important. Table 9-6 presents the frequency of appeal in each city.

The principal conclusion to be drawn from Table 9-6 is that relatively few investors in any city appeal their assessments. The appeals system may serve an important purpose by establishing the possibility of remedy for individual inequities, but the appeals can by no means alter the overall impact of the assessment system. If a system treats a certain class of properties inequitably in

Table 9-6
Frequency of Appeals by City

City	Number of Appeals	Separately Listed Parcels	Appeals as Percentage of all Parcels
Atlanta	1,500	180,000	0.8%
Baltimore	5,000	250,000	2.0
Chicago	23,000	1,300,000	1.8
Detroit	5,000	423,000	1.2
Nashville	400	136,000	0.3
Oklahoma City	30	220,000	0.0
Philadelphia	1,300	550,000	0.2
Portland	600	200,000	0.3
Providence	75	45,000	0.2
San Francisco	1,000	154,000	0.6

Notes: This refers to formal appeals only and excludes numerous requests for review that are routinely handled without use of the formal appeal procedures.
Source: Assessor Interview question 5d.

the original assessment, this class of properties will continue to be treated inequitably after appeal.

The sample evidence presented in Table 9-7 demonstrates that the investors who do make use of the appeals system are large investors. Mastering the appeal formalities requires a moderate amount of expertise, which it pays investors to acquire only if they can apply their knowledge to obtain reductions on several different properties.

Table 9-7
Frequency of Appeal by Investor Size

Investor Size	No. of Properties	No. Appealed	Percentage Appealed
Homeowner	45	2	4.4%
2 to 10 units	42	4	9.5
11 to 39 units	80	8	10.0
40 to 399 units	152	33	21.7
400 + units	71	23	32.4
Commercial	30	15	50.0
All properties	420	85	20.3

Sample: All residential and commercial properties.
Notes: Properties with appeals had assessment appeal once or more in period 1966-1970.
Source: Investor Interview question 26g, Homeowner Interview question 21b, and Property Data Sheet question 4.

Success on appeal was quite evenly distributed by investor size. Combined with the unequal distribution of appeals, the net impact of the appeals system was to improve markedly the economic position of large investors. Table 9-8 shows the ultimate disposition of investors' appeals.

Earlier chapters have made clear that the greatest property-tax burden in our sample falls on the blighted neighborhoods of Baltimore, Chicago, and Philadelphia. Since tax rates here are in greatest need of alteration, it is interesting to determine how successful the appeals systems of these cities are at adjusting assessed valuations. Table 9-9 shows that only the large investors in the blighted neighborhoods of these cities benefited from appeals.

Table 9-8

Disposition of Appeals by Investor Size, 1966-1970

Investor Size	Total Number of Properties with Appeals	Appealed but No Change in Assessment	Assessment Reduced 10% or Less	Assessment Reduced More than 10%	Appeal Unresolved
Homeowner	2	0	1	0	1
2 to 40 units	12	2	4	4	2
41 + units	56	11	15	18	12
Commercial	15	2	6	7	0
All properties	85	15	26	29	15

Sample: All residential and commercial properties with one or more appeals of assessment in the period 1966 to 1970.

Notes: Properties with appeals had assessment appealed once or more in period 1966-1970.

Source: Investor Interview question 26a, Homeowner Interview question 21b, and Property Data Sheet question 4.

Table 9-9

Disposition of Appeals in Blighted Neighborhoods of Baltimore, Chicago, and Philadelphia

Investor Size	Total Number of Properties	Properties with Appeals	Assessment Reduced 10% or Less	Assessment Reduced More than 10%	Appeal Unresolved
Homeowner	3	0	0	0	0
2 to 40 units	8	2	2	0	0
41 + units	15	11	3	5	3
All properties	26	13	5	5	3

Sample: All residential properties for the blighted neighborhoods of Baltimore, Chicago, and Philadelphia.

Notes: Properties with appeals had assessment appealed once or more in period 1966-1970.

Source: Investor Interview question 26a, Homeowner Interview question 21b, and Property Data Sheet question 4.

Conclusion

The objective of assessment is to estimate the true cash value of real-estate parcels as accurately as possible. The agreed standard for measuring assessment performance is the deviation between assessed valuations and the actual price levels at which properties change hands in legitimate sales. Deviations of assessment/sales ratios from the legislatively mandated target level may be randomly distributed or systematically distributed. In the latter case, certain classes or locations of properties are favored over others.

The evidence of this survey indicates that the most efficient means of limiting both types of dispersion is through repeated checks of neighborhood sales ratios. In those states where the state government has assumed responsibility for validating legally prescribed assessment/sales ratios, deviations from the norm seem to be less than in states where monitoring is less active. The principal price changes that occur in large cities are changes in the relative valuations of different neighborhood locations. The actual lag in reassessment behind changes in market values produces most of the serious deviations of assessment values from sales values. In principle, some of the resulting inequities can be corrected by the appeals procedure, but in practice the volume of appeals in each city is extremely small. In addition, the bias of appeals systems in favor of large investors means that assessments, after appeal, are more regressive than before appeal.

10 Property-Tax Alternatives

One objective of this study was to determine investors' and assessors' responses to various alternative methods that have been suggested for levying the property tax. In particular, we wanted to determine whether any alternatives were clearly favored over the current property tax system. This chapter discusses these alternatives and respondents' comments about them.

The Present System

Property taxes have come in for a great deal of public criticism recently. Despite this, respondents regarded the present system of taxing the market value of properties (a flat tax on land and improvements together) as preferable to most of the eight alternatives they were asked to evaluate. Even among those who objected to the present tax, several stressed that it was the unequal *application* of the tax's principles which they took exception to, rather than the principle of taxing market value. Assessors showed an overwhelming preference for the present system over all alternatives.

Table 10-1 presents the proportion of investors who considered the present system "desirable" or "very desirable," together with similar proportions for the other eight alternatives. These alternatives were:

Alternative 1: Assessing property on the basis of the present use of land without adjusting the assessed valuation to reflect improvements or physical deterioration

Alternative 2: Assessing property on the basis of the highest and best use of land only, without regard to improvements or physical deterioration or present zoning restrictions

Alternative 3: Assessing property so that land values are subject to a higher rate of taxation than improvements

Alternative 4: Determining tax liability on the basis of capitalization of a property's net income (rental receipts minus expenses for operations, maintenance, repairs, and replacement)

Alternative 5: Determining property's tax liability on the basis of a fixed proportion (e.g., 15 percent) of annual gross-rent receipts

Alternative 6: Reassessing property improvements, but offering a five-year tax abatement on the improvement

Alternative 7: Imposing higher taxes on properties that are in violation of local housing and building codes

Alternative 8: Assessing properties on the basis of their present use, but at the value they are estimated to have if in full compliance with the local codes (this approach involves a penalty for properties kept in substandard condition)

Investors showed a preference for those systems which seemed to offer tax reductions—e.g., abatements for improvement—rather than those which involved penalties—e.g., imposing higher taxes on properties in violation of housing codes. Comparison on this basis is misleading, however. Unless revenue is forthcoming from some other source, it is unlikely that a property-tax system could be adopted which lowered net tax receipts. In order to finance abatements for improvements, the overall rate structure would have to be increased. If this should occur, support for the abatement alternative doubtless would decline.

The reaction to the present tax system by neighborhood is revealing. Table 10-2 shows that opposition to the present tax system is concentrated in the blighted neighborhoods of Baltimore, Chicago, and Philadelphia, precisely those areas that suffer most from the way assessment presently is carried out. As Chapter 3 demonstrated, the blighted neighborhoods in these cities bear as much as ten times the tax burden of the upward transitional neighborhoods.

The Alternatives

Generally, investors responded to the tax alternatives as economically rational men, who favored those tax proposals which would benefit them most.

Table 10-1
Property Owners' Responses to Proposed Alternative Tax Systems (Percentage Indicating that Proposal was "Desirable" or "Very Desirable")

Alternative	Percent	Alternative	Percent
1	19.1%	6	72.4%
2	20.5	7	34.6
3	20.3	8	33.6
4	65.6	Current Method	56.6
5	50.0		

Sample: All property owners responding to question.

Notes: Figures do not add to 100 percent because each individual was permitted to recommend more than one alterantive as desirable or very desirable.

Source: Investor Interview question 29, and Homeowner Interview question 24.

Table 10-2

Property Owners' Attitudes Toward Current Assessment System, by Neighborhood and City Grouping (Percentage Indicating that Current Assessment System Was "Desirable" or "Very Undesirable")

	Baltimore Chicago Philadelphia	Atlanta Detroit Nashville Oklahoma City Portland San Francisco
Stable	60.0%	37.5%
Upward transitional	21.4	25.0
Downward transitional	75.0	31.8
Blighted	92.3	42.3
Total	61.1	34.8

Sample: All property owners responding to question.

Notes: First group contains those cities with most uneven assessment across neighborhoods. Providence is excluded from this first group because this question was not included in the pilot questionnaire.

Source: Investor Interview question 29, and Homeowner Interview question 24.

Land Taxation or a Differential Tax on Land and Improvements

These alternatives received very little support from investors. Only 20 percent found land taxation to be desirable or very desirable. Assessors on balance disliked the idea. Several claimed it would give them more discretionary power than they desired in determining assessed valuations. Investors and assessors alike felt it was preferable to leave the determination of optimal use to the market. To the extent that market values are determined by the alternative use to which land could be put, assessment on the basis of market value is a tax on land value, though the market also recognizes that the land, as presently available, is encumbered.

Others objected to assessing properties on the basis of their highest and best use because it was impossible, even among experts, to find universal agreement on what constituted optimal use. Bureaucratic determination of the value of land in optimal use would require a degree of governmental intervention in the real-estate market which investors and assessors alike found undesirable.

Tax on Net Income

This approach was a heavy favorite, especially in blighted neighborhoods where many owners claimed to have virtually zero net income. As several respondents pointed out, estimates of market value ought to be based on net income projections. Adopting a tax on the expected net-income stream would only bring pressure on the taxing authorities to levy the tax in the manner which they should be following in any event. A tax on the current year's net income would discriminate, however, against older buildings in downward transitional and blighted areas where the property's remaining economic life is shorter.

The more sophisticated investors in the sample recognized that a tax on net income easily could be abused. One large investor stated that if such a tax system were adopted his first action would be to set up dummy corporations from which he would purchase materials and furnishings. By paying himself (in another corporate capacity) excessive prices for maintenance and materials, he could reduce the net income of his rental property to zero. Several other respondents reported that a skillful investor always could show zero income for tax purposes. A tax on net income also discourages modernizing of plant and equipment, since the gains from cost reductions are partially offset by increased taxes.

Tax on Gross Income

As pointed out in Chapter 3, a tax on gross income is much more regressive than a tax on market value, when both are implemented fairly. In low-rent housing, the proportion of net to gross income tends to be lower than in high-rent housing, and the expected lifetime of the income stream is much shorter. Therefore, in low-rent housing the total net income to be gained from any current gross rent is much less—a fact which the market recognizes in lower asset prices. If the gross-rent multiplier is small in low-rent districts and large in high-rent districts, switching from a fairly administered tax on market value to a fairly administered tax on gross rents would increase the tax burden of low-rent housing and decrease the burden of luxury housing.

Despite this fact, a surprising proportion of investors in blighted neighborhoods responded favorably to a tax on gross rents. The reasons given were twofold: first, in many cities, the application of the present system is so biased against low-rent housing that blighted properties presently are paying higher percentages of gross income for property taxes than are luxury rental properties. Thus these properties clearly would benefit from the change of tax method. Second, calculating tax liability as a percentage of gross income eliminates some of the risk of the tax system for the investor. He knows that his tax bill can increase only if his receipts increase. This eliminates the cash squeeze many investors in blighted and downward transitional neighborhoods fear most—a reduction in rents accompanied by an increase in taxes.

The advantages of reduced risk can be achieved more directly, without the regressive impact of a tax on gross rent, by ensuring that the assessor keeps assessed valuations in all neighborhoods current by reducing assessments on properties which have diminished income possibilities.

The tax on either net or gross income poses some difficult conceptual and administrative problems when applied to homeowners. For owner-occupied properties an imputed rental value would have to be determined, probably based on actual rent payments for comparable homes.

Abatement for Improvements

This alternative, too, received much support.[1] Most investors treated it as a windfall gain. Because they plan to carry out improvements, many respondents stand to gain from an abatement on reassessment for improvements. We found little evidence that an abatement policy would encourage substantial upgrading that otherwise would not occur. One city in our sample had experimented with an abatement policy. Providence has granted a five year abatement for all improvements carried out on residential property in the city. To determine the incentive effect of the policy, we conducted a telephone survey of a random sample of fifty participants in the program. Of this total, only two families reported that the availability of the abatement had contributed to their decision to improve their properties. Seven other families reported that the abatement had affected the timing of the improvment. These families had carried out their improvements more rapidly than originally planned in order to take advantage of the abatement. For the most part, families reported that the abatement had not affected their decision at all. Since abatement was available, they simply took advantage of it to reduce their tax liability.

The relatively small impact of tax abatement receives confirmation from investors' responses to the question whether extension of a tax abatement and/or tax credit would induce them to undertake rehabilitation. The responses to these questions are presented in Tables 10-3 and 10-4. For many, such proposals would add to the return of already profitable rehabilitation investments. Yet, despite the self-interest of investors to respond favorably to such questions, a majority of property owners in blighted areas indicated that neither form of tax inducement would affect their plans for rehabilitation. We should note, however, that large investors responded more favorably to the prospect of tax abatements than did small investors. This conforms with other evidence that strictly economic inducements are likely to have their greatest impact on this class of investor. As we have pointed out previously, families often expressed the fear that they would be reassessed for improvements which, according to the assessor, are not assessed at all. Much of the incentive effect of a tax-abatement policy could be obtained by publishing a list of improvements which never are assessed, thus permitting an investor to determine beforehand whether the improvement he plans to make will be cause for a tax increase.

Table 10-3
Would a Five-Year Tax Abatement for Reassessment Induce Rehabilitation? (by Neighborhood and Character of Ownership)

Neighborhood	Homeowners		Small Investors 40 Units or Fewer		Large Investors 41 Units or More		Total	
	Number of Properties	Percentage "Yes"	Number of Properties	Percentage "Yes"	Number of Properties	Percentage "Yes"	Number of Properties	Percentage "Yes"
Stable	13	15.4%	18	33.3%	65	56.9%	96	46.9%
Upward transitional	8	25.0	31	54.8	50	54.0	89	51.7
Downward transitional	10	30.0	36	44.4	38	47.4	84	44.0
Blighted	8	25.0	24	12.5	52	32.7	84	26.2
All neighborhoods	39	23.1	109	38.5	205	48.3	353	42.5

Sample: All residential properties. Providence Pilot Questionnaire did not include this question.
Source: Investor Interview question 24C, Homeowner Interview question 20b.

Table 10-4
Would a Property-Tax Credit Induce Rehabilitation by Neighborhood and Character of Owner?

Neighborhood	Homeowners		Small Investors 40 Units or Fewer		Large Investors 41 Units or More		Total	
	Number of Properties	Percentage "Yes"	Number of Properties	Percentage "Yes"	Number of Properties	Percentage "Yes"	Number of Properties	Percentage "Yes"
Stable	13	18.2%	18	33.3%	65	53.8%	96	44.8%
Upward transitional	8	37.5	31	51.9	50	58.0	89	50.7
Downward transitional	10	30.0	36	50.0	38	44.7	84	45.2
Blighted	8	50.0	24	37.5	52	61.5	84	53.5
All neighborhoods	39	30.8	109	42.2	205	55.1	353	48.4

Sample: All residential properties. Providence Questionnaire did not include this question.
Source: Investor Interview question 24d, Homeowner Interview question 20c.

While the granting of tax abatements or tax credits might generate a significant amount of upgrading of properties, the long-run effects of such a policy are far from clear. In many older cities, improvements to existing properties constitute a greater proportion of total residential investment than new construction. Given the fact that one of the major criticisms of the property tax is the slow growth of the tax base, it might very well prove self-defeating if a city were to write off upgrading and rehabilitation as a source of tax-base expansion by exempting it from tax liability. The higher rates of taxation that would have to be borne by other property owners in order to generate the same growth in tax revenue would discourage new construction and accelerate abandonment of marginal properties. Whether the total effect of such a policy would be to increase the net volume of all housing investment is a difficult question that could be answered only by a complete model of the housing market.

Tax Penalty for Code Violation

Both assessors and investors overwhelmingly opposed higher taxes on properties which were in violation of local housing and building codes. The reason for most of this opposition was based on the fact that some properties, particularly in blighted areas, simply do not generate enough rental income to support the provision of standard units. As pointed out in Chapter 4, strict enforcement of local codes in this case would lead to abandonment. In addition, where insufficient rental demand is not the underlying cause of substandard housing, municipalities already possess the necessary legal powers to correct code violations.

Overhauling the Property-Tax System

While homeowners, investors, and assessors were explicitly asked to comment on the foregoing alternatives, other tax reforms were often mentioned voluntarily. As Table 10-5 makes clear, these responses fall into four main categories.

Foremost among investor concerns was the need to substitute some other major source of revenue for the property tax. Fear of increasing rates of taxation disturbed most respondents more than the method of assessment. While it is beyond the scope of this study to suggest alternative sources of municipal revenue, federal assumption of a larger portion of the costs of welfare and education seems the most promising long-run solution to the increasing burden of property taxation.

The second most frequently volunteered response concerned the administration of the property tax. Investors in several cities complained that the

Table 10-5
Investor Complaints Regarding Property Taxes

Item	Number of Respondents Volunteering Complaint
Lower property tax by substituting other forms of taxation	29
Improve administration of tax	24
Make assessment more sensitive to market or income changes	23
Too many tax-exempt properties, or too large concession to federally subsidized projects	15

Sample: All investors, excluding single-family homeowners.

Notes: Question 28 read "What specific changes, if any, in the property tax and its administration could you recommend to encourage more landlords to keep their property in good repair." While this open ended question brought a variety of responses, four common themes appeared.

Source: Investor Interview question 28.

appeals procedure, especially at the first level, was unprofessional, since investors typically had to present their appeal to a board of assessors, composed of the same men who had determined the assessed valuation in the first place. There were also a considerable number of complaints by investors about the inability to get straight answers regarding the policy for reassessing improvements.

A significant number of investors complained that assessments strayed too far from market value. Respondents urged that the assessors pay more attention to market value, and less to their formulas for replacement costs and depreciation. Finally, several investors complained that they were being forced to pay higher taxes to pay for the provision of services to tax-exempt properties and properties with special tax concessions.

11   Reforming the Property-Tax System

This study has found that in many cities there is a systematic neighborhood bias in assessment practices and general confusion over the workings of the property-tax system. This can adversely affect the functioning of both center-city housing markets and the operation of programs designed to improve housing conditions in the cities.

For these and other reasons, such as widespread concern about the interjurisdictional equity of taxing local property wealth, the property tax has come under increased attack. Yet, because of the property tax's long history as a successful revenue-raising device, it seems unlikely that its role in state and local financing will be substantially diminished in the near future. In November 1972, voters in several states soundly defeated a wide range of proposals to reduce or eliminate reliance on property taxation. In March 1973, the Supreme Court refused to rule that the use of the local property tax to finance public schools violated the "Equal Protection Clause" of the Constitution. The evidence presented in Chapter 10 indicates that real-estate investors also are reluctant to see the property tax replaced by any of the most commonly advocated alternatives.

Given the likelihood that municipalities will continue to depend upon the property tax as their principal source of locally raised revenue, the major public policy question is, "what reforms in the current property-tax system would make it more equitable and more effective?" rather than, "what new tax sources should replace the property-tax system?" This book has identified several targets for reform. In the first place, the systematic bias of assessments by neighborhood makes the property tax in many cities a more regressive tax instrument than it need be. As previously indicated, in the older cities of our sample it was not unusual for properties in blighted neighborhoods to bear an effective tax rate ten times as great as properties in the upward transitional neighborhoods of the same city. Assuming that any or all of these tax differentials are passed along to tenants, this assessment bias is distinctly prejudicial to the poor and in most cases to the black population as well.

Of equal importance are the indications that assessment bias can represent an important contributing element to neighborhood blight. To the extent that landlords must absorb part of the property-tax burden themselves (and most owners in blighted neighborhoods reported that the high vacancy rates there made it impossible to pass on all tax increases), the higher effective tax rates that result from overassessment will substantially diminish a property's cash flow. In earlier chapters, we presented some evidence indicating that small investors,

119

especially, have difficulty obtaining external financing for repairs or rehabilitation, for which reason their investments in a property often are constrained by the cash flow which the parcel generates. In this situation, any increase in an important cost factor like property taxes that places a squeeze on cash flow will show up directly in reduced expenditures on maintenance, repairs, and upgrading.

The fact that parcels generate a marginal or negative cash flow also means that their market value will have fallen close to zero. The collapse of the market for low-income housing in the blighted neighborhoods of several cities has left in its wake a number of bitter, disillusioned investors who want only to liquidate their holdings but are unable to find buyers for them. In Chapter 4 we argued that there is reason to expect that the supply of housing in low-income areas could be improved if a substantial number of properties were to change hands from absentee, white landlords to new owners who were not saddled by a history of large capital losses and who understood better the nature of housing demand in the low-income community. A one-time equalization of effective property-tax rates then would have an added benefit. By reducing the operating costs on marginal parcels, lower property-tax payments would augment the cash flow which these properties could generate, thereby increasing their market value. Our survey of investor attitudes suggests that if this should happen, a large number of owners would take advantage of the opportunity to sell out, thereby substantially altering the character of property ownership in blighted neighborhoods.

In short one of the most urgent tax "reforms" is to implement what is already legally prescribed, by equalizing effective tax rates across neighborhoods within the same city. This neighborhood equalization of effective property tax rates would make the tax burden more equitable and contribute to the upgrading of blighted areas.

Equalization of the Property-Tax Base Across Jurisdictions

In Chapter 8 we considered the effect of another popular property-tax reform proposal—the equalization of tax bases, either among the jurisdictions of a metropolitan area or among all the tax jurisdictions in a state. This plan has been dubbed "power equalization" by lawyers, since it would give every jurisdiction the power to raise equal revenues if they levied equal property-tax rates. A case may be made that the principle of "equal dollars for equal tax effort" represents the fairest possible tax system, and that therefore power equalization should be adopted, whatever its implications for different jurisdictions. However, we attempted to show in Chapter 8 that insofar as the purpose of tax equalization is to aid the fiscally distressed central cities, it is impossible to say, except on the basis of case-by-case scrutiny, whether tax-base equalization will achieve this end or not. In some cities (we cited the example of Baltimore) tax-base equalization would represent a substantial shot in the arm for the central city. In other cities (we cited Detroit) equalization of tax bases across jurisdictions would destroy the one advantage the central city presently enjoys in its efforts to compete with the suburbs for middle- and upper-income residents. While it is perhaps discouraging that it should be so, there seems to be no set rule to determine whether central cities are richer or poorer, in terms of average per capita real property, than the other jurisdictions in a state. In these circumstances, the route to fiscal relief for the cities would seem to lie in arrangements for spreading the costs of certain basic city services, like police protection and welfare, health and schooling, among a larger population, not by efforts to spread the tax base over the entire metropolitan area or state.

The Role of the States

The states have a critical role to play in reform of the existing property-tax system even if a shift to uniform statewide taxation is not carried out. This role requires the state to monitor local assessment performance and encourage the use of efficient assessment techniques.

Throughout this study we offered evidence that local assessment procedures are most effective and equitable in cities like Portland and San Francisco where the state government exercises considerable control over local assessment practices. In both of these cases the state government has the authority to take effective steps to see that the assessment process is carried out uniformly. In Oregon, for instance, the state can order an independent reappraisal of all local properties if assessment-sales ratios get too far out of line. As a last resort, it can pay for the expense of such a reappraisal by withholding a portion of the state cigarette-tax revenue normally returned to the counties. In California, the State Board of Equalization not only carries out periodic evaluations of the policies and procedures of local assessors' offices, but has been active in encouragement of new appraisal techniques such as the use of computerized mass-assessment programs. Whatever mechanisms are used to make assessments, this study has suggested that the most serious defect of the present assessment systems is its inability to keep abreast with changes in neighborhood-wide market values. Simple, annual assessment/sales ratio checks, by neighborhood, could do much to remove the most flagrant inequities in the assessment system.

The evidence reported in this study also confirms findings reported elsewhere that the assessment appeals system as presently operated does little to equalize tax burdens. A relatively small number of persons avail themselves of the appeal mechanism, and these by and large are the professional investors who least require assistance. Ironically, then, the impact of the appeals system is to make property taxes more inequitable than they would be otherwise. The scope for state initiative in instituting an effective appeals system obviously is very great.

Finally, the role of the federal government should be to reinforce reform efforts by the states. Through technical assistance and the development of model statutes, or through federal incentive grants, the national government can help bring about a reform of the current property-tax system.

Appendixes

Appendix A: Definition of Terms

Neighborhood

While the concept of neighborhood is subject to varying definitions, for this study we have used an operational definition based on property and land values of the structures in the neighborhood. All characteristics which determine the market value of a property are reflected in its price, e.g., age and type of structure, proximity to job location, and quality of neighborhood services. The use of the market price of structures to define and distinguish different neighborhoods has four important advantages:

a. It establishes a measurable criterion-price—which is ascertainable.
b. It is unambiguous.
c. It is the criterion which real estate investors and local planners and officials use.
d. It is the neighborhood price trend, more than any other phenomenon, which determines the investment strategies of realtors.

The four neighborhood types were selected primarily in terms of relative market prices. But because there is a strong relation between relative market prices and certain socio-economic and land use characteristics, the neighborhood selection was also supplemented by this type of data. The following definitions were used for neighborhood selection.

A. Blighted Neighborhood

Neighborhoods where property values are steady at a low rate or sinking toward zero. Blighted neighborhoods usually are characterized by a large proportion of sub-standard and vacant dwellings; mixed residential, commercial, commercial and/or industrial use; relatively low rent levels; high densities and minority population.

B. Upward and Downward Transitional Neighborhoods

Upward transitional neighborhoods are those where property values are increasing at an above average rate. Downward transitional neighborhoods are where values are declining. Transitional neighborhoods are in the process of

125

change: population is changing, there is a mix of multi-family and single unit residences, standard and substandard dwellings, property conversions and some mixed zoning.

C. Stable Neighborhoods

Stable neighborhoods are those where property values are constant at a high level or increasing at the city-wide average rate.

Our aim was to select neighborhood boundaries in such a way as to form homogeneous housing submarkets. We found that homogeneous housing submarkets often coincide with geographic or topographic features, governmental program definitions or historical demarcations. Sometimes the degree of homogeneity was surprising. In Chicago, for example, we found neighborhoods where the housing stock was quite uniform, built at the same time with similar materials, and now undergoing similar quality and price changes.

Other Definitions Used

In addition to the definitions needed to operationalize the selection of the neighborhoods and sample properties, other definitions were established for the purpose of the study.

Building Quality Level

An overall measure of housing quality developed by measuring services provided such as janitorial and managerial, as well as the state of the physical plant. This study examines change in building quality level over the years 1966-1970.

Calculation of Value Appreciation or Depreciation

Present sales price minus the purchase price plus the cost of any capital improvements (moderate renovation and/or extensive reconstruction—see definitions under "Rehabilitation"). This calculation is based on current prices.

Cash Flow

Actual gross rent collected less all cash outlays including debt service, property taxes, maintenance and operations.

Effective Tax Rate

Tax payments as a percentage of current market value of the property.

Gross Rent Multiplier

Market value of the property as a percentage of gross rent. In the case of owner occupied multiple structures, the gross rent figure includes an imputed rent for the owner's unit. The imputed rent is equal to the market rent charged for a similar unit in the same neighborhood. A similar imputation is needed for the provision of apartment space to a janitor, or building manager in lieu of salary.

Long-term Investment

Investments which have an expected or actual term of five years or more.

Mill Rate or Millage

Tax rates expressed as amount per 1000 dollars of assessed valuation.

Number of Properties Owned

Total number of properties owned outright or in conjunction with others, including properties being purchased under various financing arrangements.

Operating Expenses

All expenses which require a cash outlay and are deductible under Federal Internal Revenue Service regulations. This excludes mortgage amortization and capital improvements.

Private Market Real Estate

All properties except those owned by non-profit or by limited profit entities operating with the assistance of such programs as 221(d)3 or 236.

Rehabilitation

All properties except those owned by non-profit or by limited profit entities operating with the assistance of such programs as 221 (d)3 or 236.

(a) Minor Repair

Those requiring only a paint-up/fix-up or decoration of interior and exterior walls, ceilings, and floors.

(b) Moderate Renovation

Those needing "renovation" which includes, in addition to painting such work as leveling floors, straightening partitions, replacing doors and windows, plus modernizing heating, plumbing, and electrical systems, and resurfacing (paneling, plastering, new siding, etc.) interior or exterior walls, ceilings, floors or roof.

(c) Extensive Reconstruction

Those needing a "gut" job—all the items in renovation plus removal of partitions and major changes in floor plans, roofs, new interior walls, etc.

Residential Rental Properties

All buildings which are exclusively residential rental and those which are mixed commercial and residential rental.

Short-term Investment

Investments which have an expected or actual term of five years or less.

Single Family Homeowner

An individual who held no other real estate other than his own home.

Appendix B: City Housing and Population Characteristics, 1960-1970

Table B-1
Atlanta Summary

	1970	1960
I. *Housing Characteristics*		
A. Total Housing Units	170,892	153,677
1. Percentage one-unit structures	49.3	58.6
2. Percentage two- to four-unit structures	–	21.8
3. Percentage five-unit structures or larger	–	19.6
B. Total Black Occupied Units	71,166	47,939
1. Percentage owner-occupied units	37.4	29.3
C. Total Owner-Occupied Units	66,823	66,504
1. Percentage one-unit structures	92.6	91.4
2. Percentage two- to four-unit strucures	–	7.9
3. Percentage five-unit structures of larger	–	0.6
4. Homeowner vacancy rate	1.2	2.3
5. Median value single-family, owner-occupied	$17,200	$12,000
D. Total Occupied Rental Units	95,489	79,449
1. Percentage one-unit structures	21.0	32.8
2. Percentage two- to four-unit structures	–	32.6
3. Percentage five-unit structures or larger	–	34.6
4. Renter vacancy rate	5.9	4.9
5. Median contract rent	$80	$54
E. Units Built Before 1939		70,365
II. *Population Characteristics*		
A. Total Population	516,993	487,455
1. White	240,551	300,635
2. Nonwhite	256,442	186,820
B. Median Income	–	$5,758
III. *Neighborhoods Sampled*		
A. Blighted	Pittsburg/Vine City	
B. Downward Transitional	West End	
C. Upward Transitional	Uptown/Inman Park	
D. Stable	Peachtree Hills	

Table B-2
Baltimore Summary

	1970	1960
I. *Housing Characteristics*		
A. Total Housing Units	305,464	289,734
1. Percentage one-unit structures	61.1	63.0
2. Percentage two- to four-unit structures	–	26.4
3. Percentage five-unit structures or larger	–	10.6
B. Total Black Occupied Units	34,299	27,628
1. Percentage owner-occupied units	30.1	34.3
C. Total Owner-Occupied Units	128,763	149,668
1. Percentage one-unit structures	90.7	91.2
2. Percentage two- to four-unit structures	–	5.2
3. Percentage five-unit structures or larger	–	3.6
4. Homeowner vacancy rate	0.9	1.4
5. Median value single-family, owner-occupied	$10,000	$9,000
D. Total Occupied Rental Units	160,586	125,929
1. Percentage one-unit structures	39.6	48.2
2. Percentage two- to four-unit structures	–	35.4
3. Percentage five-unit structures or larger	–	17.4
4. Renter vacancy rate	5.8	6.4
5. Median contract rent	$90	$64
E. Units Built Before 1939		199,711
II. *Population Characteristics*		
A. Total Population	905,759	939,024
1. White	479,837	610,608
2. Nonwhite	425,922	328,416
B. Median Income		$6,185
III. *Neighborhoods Sampled*		
A. Blighted		East Baltimore
B. Downward Transitional		Patterson Park
C. Upward Transitional		Bolton Hill
D. Stable		Guilford

Table B-3
Chicago Summary

	1970	1960
I. *Housing Characteristics*		
A. Total Housing Units	1,208,327	1,212,264
1. Percentage one-unit structures	23.8	24.0
2. Percentage two- to four-unit structures	–	36.9
3. Percentage five-unit structures or larger	–	39.1
B. Total Black Occupied Units	314,640	233,263
1. Percentage owner-occupied units	23.6	15.7
C. Total Owner-Occupied Units	396,357	396,727
1. Percentage one-unit structures	51.6	58.4
2. Percentage two- to four-unit structures		35.9
3. Percentage five-unit structures or larger	–	5.7
4. Homeowner vacancy rate	0.6	0.6
5. Median value single-family, owner-occupied	$21,200	$18,000
D. Total Occupied Rental Units	741,497	760,682
1. Percentage one-unit structures	7.2	7.2
2. Percentage two- to four-unit structures	–	37.9
3. Percentage five-unit structures or larger	–	54.9
4. Renter vacancy rate	6.7	5.2
5. Median contract rent	$108	$78
E. Units Built Before 1939		841,524
II. *Population Characteristics*		
A. Total Population	3,366,957	3,550,404
1. White	2,207,767	2,712,748
2. Nonwhite	1,159,190	837,656
B. Median Income		$7,342
III. *Neighborhoods Sampled*		
A. Blighted	Woodlawn	
B. Downward Transitional	Logan Square	
C. Upward Transitional	Lincoln Park	
D. Stable	Hyde Park/Norwood Park	

Table B-4
Detroit Summary

	1970	1960
I. *Housing Characteristics*		
A. Total Housing Units	529,043	552,050
1. Percentage one-unit structures	53.9	60.1
2. Percentage two- to four-unit structures	−	22.9
3. Percentage five-unit structures or larger	−	17.0
B. Total Black Occupied Units	192,902	129,643
1. Percentage owner-occupied units	51.1	39.0
C. Total Owner-Occupied Units	298,624	299,472
1. Percentage one-unit structures	83.4	86.8
2. Percentage two- to four-unit structures	−	12.4
3. Percentage five-unit structures or larger	−	0.8
4. Homeowner vacancy rate	1.5	0.9
5. Median value single-family, owner-occupied	$15,600	$12,000
D. Total Occupied Rental Units	199,129	215,365
1. Percentage one-unit structures	15.4	28.7
2. Percentage two- to four-unit structures	−	35.5
3. Percentage five-unit structures or larger	−	36.8
4. Renter vacancy rate	9.2	11.5
5. Median contract rent	$80	$64
E. Units Built Before 1939		202,212
II. *Population Characteristics*		
A. Total Population	1,511,482	1,670,144
1. White	838,877	1,182,970
2. Nonwhite	672,605	487,174
B. Median Income	−	$6,825
III. *Neighborhoods Sampled*		
A. Blighted		John R.
B. Downward Transitional		Jefferson/Mack
C. Upward Transitional		Cadillac
D. Stable		Palmer Park

Table B-5
Nashville Summary

	1970	1960
I. *Housing Characteristics*		
A. Total Housing Units	147,226	120,474
1. Percentage one-unit structures	67.7	76.7
2. Percentage two- to four-unit structures	–	15.5
3. Percentage five-unit structures or larger	–	7.8
B. Total Black Occupied Units	24,222	20,175
1. Percentage owner-occupied units	39.7	36.6
C. Total Owner-Occupied Units	83,706	69,865
1. Percentage one-unit structures	91.8	93.3
2. Percentage two- to four-unit structures	–	6.4
3. Percentage five-unit structures or larger	–	0.4
4. Homeowner vacancy rate	0.9	0.4
5. Median value single-family, owner-occupied	$15,800	$10,800
D. Total Occupied Rental Units	56,705	44,770
1. Percentage one-unit structures	35.8	51.1
2. Percentage two- to four-unit structures	–	29.7
3. Percentage five-unit structures or larger	–	19.1
4. Renter vacancy rate	7.1	5.1
5. Median contract rent	$81	$48
E. Units Built Before 1939		24,951
II. *Population Characteristics*		
A. Total Population	348,003	399,743
1. White	358,765	322,911
2. Nonwhite	89,238	76,832
B. Median Income		$5,059
III. *Neighborhoods Sampled*		
A. Blighted		Sulpher Dell
B. Downward Transitional		Fisk Park
C. Upward Transitional		Edgehill
D. Stable		S.W. Nashville

Table B-6
Oklahoma City Summary

	1970	1960
I. *Housing Characteristics*		
A. Total Housing Units	138,378	114,513
1. Percentage one-unit structures	76.3	82.5
2. Percentage two- to four-unit structures	–	82.5
3. Percentage five-unit structures or larger	–	8.7
B. Total Black Occupied Units	14,470	11,871
1. Percentage owner-occupied units	55.4	47.3
C. Total Owner-Occupied Units	81,908	66,957
1. Percentage one-unit structures	95.8	96.9
2. Percentage two- to four-unit structures	–	2.5
3. Percentage five-unit structures or larger	–	0.7
4. Homeowner vacancy rate	1.9	2.3
5. Median value single-family, owner-occupied	$13,100	$9,800
D. Total Occupied Rental Units	45.037	40,097
1. Percentage one-unit structures	47.7	62.4
2. Percentage two- to four-unit structures	–	18.7
3. Percentage five-unit structures or larger	–	18.9
4. Renter vacancy rate	13.1	8.2
5. Median contract rent	$74	$51
E. Units Built Before 1939		52,953
II. *Population Characteristics*		
A. Total Population	366,481	324,253
1. White	307,628	281,971
2. Nonwhite	58,853	42,282
B. Median Income	–	$5,601
III. *Neighborhoods Sampled*		
A. Blighted	John Kennedy	
B. Downward Transitional	Capital Hill	
C. Upward Transitional	Historical District	
D. Stable	N.W. Oklahoma City	

Table B-7
Philadelphia Summary

	1970	1960
I. *Housing Characteristics*		
A. Total Housing Units	673,390	647,911
1. Percentage one-unit structures	66.5	73.6
2. Percentage two- to four-unit structures	–	15.1
3. Percentage five-unit structures or larger	–	11.3
B. Total Black Occupied Units	194,955	149,137
1. Percentage owner-occupied units	47.4	43.0
C. Total Owner-Occupied Units	383,630	381,339
1. Percentage one-unit structures	93.3	94.7
2. Percentage two- to four-unit structures	–	4.6
3. Percentage five-unit structures or larger	–	0.7
4. Homeowner vacancy rate	1.0	1.3
5. Median value single-family, owner-occupied	$10,700	$8,700
D. Total Occupied Rental Units	258,515	234,425
1. Percentage one-unit structures	29.6	42.2
2. Percentage two- to four-unit structures	–	30.6
3. Percentage five-unit structures or larger	–	27.2
4. Renter vacancy rate	5.6	6.7
5. Median contract rent	$76	$56
E. Units Built Before 1939		505,324
II. *Population Characteristics*		
A. Total Population	1.948,609	2.002,512
1. White	1,278,717	1,467,479
2. Nonwhite	669,892	535,033
B. Median Income		$6,433
III. *Neighborhoods Sampled*		
A. Blighted	Lower North Philadelphia	
B. Downward Transitional	South West Philadelphia	
C. Upward Transitional	Queens Village	
D. Stable	South Philadelphia	

Table B-8
Portland Summary

	1970	1960
I. *Housing Characteristics*		
A. Total Housing Units	152,043	142,777
1. Percentage one-unit structures	66.8	68.4
2. Percentage two- to four-unit structures	–	7.6
3. Percentage five-unit structures or larger	–	20.5
B. Total Black Occupied Units	6,541	6,101
1. Percentage owner-occupied units	47.1	49.3
C. Total Owner-Occupied Units	81,930	83,231
1. Percentage one-unit structures	95.5	96.4
2. Percentage two- to four-unit structures	–	2.6
3. Percentage five-unit structures or larger	–	1.0
4. Homeowner vacancy rate	0.8	1.3
5. Median value single-family, owner-occupied	$14,400	$10,800
D. Total Occupied Rental Units	63,152	51,625
1. Percentage one-unit structures	32.5	32.6
2. Percentage two- to four-unit structures	–	15.7
3. Percentage five-unit structures or larger	–	51.8
4. Renter vacancy rate	6.8	8.4
5. Median contract rent	$91	$60
E. Units Built Before 1939		87,015
II. *Population Characteristics*		
A. Total Population	382,619	372,776
1. White	352,635	351,757
2. Nonwhite	29,984	20,919
B. Median Income		$6,340
III. *Neighborhoods Sampled*		
A. Blighted		Albina
B. Downward Transitional		Brooklyn
C. Upward Transitional		Couch
D. Stable		Hollywood

Table B-9
Providence Summary

	1970	1960
I. *Housing Characteristics*		
A. Total Housing Units	121,798	121,310
1. Percentage one-unit structures	21.9	24.6
2. Percentage two- to four-unit structures	–	58.1
3. Percentage five-unit structures or larger	–	17.3
B. Total Black Occupied Units	5,031	3,530
1. Percentage owner-occupied units	18.9	17.1
C. Total Owner-Occupied Units	114,762	113,995
1. Percentage one-unit structures	55.4	53.5
2. Percentage two- to four-unit structures	–	44.3
3. Percentage five-unit structures or larger	–	2.2
4. Homeowner vacancy rate	0.7	1.3
5. Median value single-family, owner-occupied	$17,000	$12,000
D. Total Occupied Rental Units	58,883	60,966
1. Percentage one-unit structures	5.1	9.4
2. Percentage two- to four-unit structures	–	58.7
3. Percentage five-unit structures or larger	–	31.9
4. Renter vacancy rate	7.0	7.1
5. Median contract rent	$63	$40
E. Units Built Before 1939		60,573
II. *Population Characteristics*		
A. Total Population	179,213	207,498
1. White	161,338	195,525
2. Nonwhite	17,875	11,973
B. Median Income		$5,632
III. *Neighborhoods Sampled*		
A. Blighted	South Providence	
B. Downward Transitional	Smith Hill	
C. Upward TRansitional	College Hill/Fox Point	
D. Stable	East Providence	

Table B-10
San Francisco Summary

	1970	1960
I. *Housing Characteristics*		
A. Total Housing Units	310,364	309,671
1. Percentage one-unit structures	33.7	37.0
2. Percentage two- to four-unit structures	–	22.8
3. Percentage five-unit structures or larger	–	40.2
B. Total Black Occupied Units	32,500	41,612
1. Percentage-owner occupied units	25.3	24.9
C. Total Owner-Occupied Units	97,036	102,141
1. Percentage one-unit structures	80.1	86.6
2. Percentage two- to four-unit structures	–	15.7
3. Percentage five-unit structures or larger	–	3.7
4. Homeowner vacancy rate	0.7	0.7
5. Median value single-family, owner-occupied	$28,100	$17,300
D. Total Occupied Rental Units	198,138	189,834
1. Percentage one-unit structures	12.6	13.5
2. Percentage two- to four-unit structures	–	26.4
3. Percentage five-unit structures or larger	–	60.1
4. Renter vacancy rate	4.7	6.6
5. Median contract rent	$128	$68
E. Units Built Before 1939		233,093
II. *Population Characteristics*		
A. Total Population	715,674	740,316
1. White	511,186	604,403
2. Nonwhite	204,488	135,913
B. Median Income		$7,147
III. *Neighborhoods Sampled*		
A. Blighted	Western Edition/Hunter's Point	
B. Downward Transitional	Mission Dolores/Haight-Filmore	
C. Upward Transitional	Marina/Pacific Heights	
D. Stable	Sunset/Richamond	

Appendix C: City-State Statutes

Atlanta, Georgia

The Tax.[1] The 159 counties in Georgia constitute the property-tax units. Property is taxed at the sum of the state, county, municipal, and school rates. Although the state still has the power to receive a portion of the property taxes, its recent share has been negligible (one-quarter mill).

Property Subject to Tax. Both real and tangible personal property is subject to tax unless exempt. Family homesteads are exempt up to $2,000 from state and county taxes and household property up to $300 is exempt from all taxes. In addition there is a state and county exemption of $10,000 for disabled veterans and $4,000 for persons sixty-five or older with incomes not exceeding $4,000.

Assessment. Property owners must file an annual return of their property which is to be listed at fair market value. Property is assessed at 40 percent of fair market value (although municipalities are not bound by this ratio). The tax assessors are not elected in Georgia. The county tax receiver assesses property that has been omitted or grossly undervalued. In addition town or city assessors assess and value property for municipal taxation subject to appeal to the municipal board of tax appeals. Returns submitted by the tax receiver are examined by the county board of tax assessors. The State Revenue Commissioner then equalizes assessments of property by classes among the counties and by classes within a county.

A recent court decision (*McLennan vs Undercofler*, Fulton Superior Court, No. B-14129, August 31, 1965 (CCH Ga. 200-135), appeal dismissed 221 Ga. 6.3, 146 S.E. 2d 635 (1966), supplemental order, March 14, 1966 (CCH Ga. 200-146)) has ordered equalization among the counties. To the extent that the courts have entered the equalization area, it should provide motivation for the state to enforce its statutory requirements.

In 1970, Fulton County hired an outside appraisal firm to help them perform a county-wide reassessment. Although this task has been completed, the utilization of the new assessments has been tied up by court action. Principal opponents claimed, among other things, that the manner in which the reassessment was conducted failed to permit owners adequate opportunity to contest valuations before they were established.

Restrictions on Tax Power. County, school district, and nonhome charter municipalities are subject to constitutional and statutory tax-rate limitations. The rate for counties is five mills including debt service. For noncity school districts the limitation is twenty mills exclusive of debt service. These limitations may be exceeded only by voter approval. Since Atlanta is a charter municipality, it is subject only to the county limitation.

1970 Tax Rates for Atlanta

Atlanta City and Fulton County $65.22 per $1000

Assessments targeted at 40 percent of actual value.

Baltimore, Maryland

The Tax.[2] Each of Maryland's twenty-three counties is an administrative unit in the assessment and collection of taxes for state and county purposes. Baltimore City is also treated as the equivalent of a county so the total number of assessing areas is twenty-four. Because it has a small number of relatively large assessment areas, Maryland can be considered one of the more progressive states from an administrative point of view. The state's portion of property-tax revenues is small (approximately 4 percent).

Property Subject to Tax. Real and tangible personal property is taxable and intangible personal property is usually exempt. Exemptions are not numerous compared to other states. The primary ones related to housing are: (1) a state-wide exemption of the house and lot of disabled veterans and (2) a tax credit of the lesser of 50 percent of the assessed property value or $4,000 for all persons over 65 or disabled with incomes of not over $5,000 per year. The city of Baltimore also has the power to exempt from all taxes levied by the city any new industry or business it is trying to attract.

Assessment. The valuation concept required is full cash value which is current value less an allowance for inflation; the legal standard rate of evaluation is 100 percent. While the state laws do not specifically require uniformity with respect to owners of the same class of property, the above standard may be interpreted to do so. The City Charter of Baltimore specifically requires uniformity.

In line with its relatively progressive structure, the property tax in Maryland is administered by appointed assessors. The assessing body in Baltimore is the Department of Assessments of Baltimore City, with appeals going to the Board of Municipal and Zoning Appeals. Certain classes of property not assessed at the local level are handled by the State Department of Assessments and Taxation, with appeals going to the Maryland Tax Court.[3] The director of the State Department of Assessments and Taxation is required to conduct biennial surveys of assessment ratios of assessed value to sales prices and/or appraised values.[4] In 1968 the ratio of assessment to actual value ranged from 48.2 percent in Garrett County to 58.4 percent in Baltimore City. This is a county average and individual properties in a given county may vary considerably around the mean. Although the law requires annual review of assessable real property and reassessment whenever a change in value is disclosed, the procedure for state-wide equalization is not defined.

The law requires corporations to file returns with the State Department of Assessments and Taxation, but individual returns are filed only when called for.

Restrictions on Tax Power. Maryland has no general constitutional and statutory restrictions on local power to raise property tax revenue. The Charter of the City of Baltimore[5] precludes the city from certain kinds of taxing power, including the imposition of taxes on income, gasolines, and motor vehicle registration.

1970 Tax Rate for Baltimore

$55.20 per $1,000 assessed value

Assessment targeted at 60 percent of actual value.

Chicago, Illinois

The Tax.[6] A large amount of local control is present in the property-tax system of Illinois as evidenced by the presence of over 1,400 primary assessing areas. This specialized autonomy with hundreds of overlapping districts makes it very difficult for the property owner to find out where his tax money is going and how it is used. Across the state the township is the principal unit for tax purposes. The rate in each area is the aggregate required for county, township, municipal, school, and special district purposes. The state receives no portion of the property tax.

Property Subject to Tax. All real and personal property is subject to tax unless specifically exempt. Intangible personal property is also theoretically taxed at the same rates as tangible property, but it has been customary to assess intangible property of individuals at lower values. Principal exemptions include: (1) household furniture and one automobile, (2) a $1,500 homestead tax credit for any dwelling owned *or* occupied by persons over 65 years of age, and (3) homesteads up to $15,000 for disabled veterans.

Assessment. The Constitution requires that the property tax be paid in proportion to a property's fair cash value.[7] Although the typical unit of tax control is the township, in Cook County an elected county assessor is responsible for assessments in Chicago and for supervision of assessors outside the city. A State Department of Local Government Affairs is required to equalize assessments among the counties, but not among classes, districts, or individuals.

In line with the popular notion that it is unfair to tax non-income-producing property at the same level of market value as income producing properties, wide discrepancies exist within individual counties. These discrepancies seem to be based more on an ability to pay basis than an evaluation of the amount of services obtained from the community. For example, one- and two-family homes will be assessed at 30 percent of value, multifamily flats at a higher level, and commercial property at close to true market value. This discrimination is carried over to personal property tax which is usually only collected from businesses.

Cook County is divided into four assessment districts with assessments subject to equalization in the same manner as counties. A multiplier is used to bring all assessed values in a county or district up to the state norm. This multiplier for Cook County in 1970 was 1.59. Real property is assessed each year in only one Cook County district. In the other three Cook County Districts and most other Illinois counties, assessment takes place quadrennially unless improvements are made or property is damaged. Equalization also takes place only every four years. In Cook County the county assessor has permitted listing of personal property at less than full value. Lists of personal property are filed with the county assessor only when he requests them. Any appeals of assessments are handled by the County Board of Appeals.

Restrictions on Tax Power. Tax rates for all primary assessing areas are subject to state constitutional or statutory limits. The limits are usually based on population size of the area and do not include debt servicing. The only exception to this general rule is that there is no municipality limit for Chicago. Otherwise, for example, the Cook County rate limit is 7.5 mills and the school district limit 15 mills. Taxation beyond these limits is provided only by specific voter approval. Individual assessing area limitations encourage the continual formation of new taxing districts.[8]

The 1970 Tax Rate for Chicago

$68.90 per $1,000 assessed value

Assessment nominally targeted at 100 percent of actual value.

Detroit, Michigan

The Tax.[9] The state of Michigan has just under 1,500 primary property-tax assessing areas. In this respect it can be compared to Illinois, which also has large numbers of overlapping tax districts. The township and the city are the principal units in property assessment. Property is taxed at the aggregate of county, township, municipal school, and other district rates. The state receives no revenue from the property tax.

Property Subject to Tax. All tangible and intangible property is subject to tax unless expressly exempt. Principal exemptions include: (1) clothes, (2) household furniture, provisions, and fuel up to $5,000, (3) personal business property up to $500, (4) homesteads of persons over sixty-five up to $2,500 if their income is less than $6,000, and (5) certain homestead exemptions for soldiers and pensioned or disabled veterans.

Assessment. Property is assessed on the basis of 50 percent of true cash value.[10] In 1970 a state equalization factor of 1.05 was applied to all property assessments in the city of Detroit. A City Board of Review hears all appeals. Further appeals may be taken to the State Tax Commission whose decision is final and cannot be taken to the county.[11] Counties exercise little supervision over the township and city assessors other than performing a yearly equalization. The State Board of Equalization has been abolished. Appeals from equalization by the County Board of Supervisors are also heard at the state level by the State Tax Commission. "The State Tax Commission shall have the same authority to consider and pass upon the action and determination of the Board of Supervisors in equalizing said valuations as it has to consider complaints relative to the assessment and taxation of property."[12] Local tax assessors are either elected or appointed, depending on the city. Assessors have the power to demand a listing of any taxable property. This return if requested must be accompanied by a sworn statement as to its validity. The city of Detroit requires this property-tax return annually.

Restrictions on Tax Power. The Michigan constitution specifies an overall tax limitation on the sum of all nonmunicipal (charter) taxation of 1.5 percent of assessed value. This limitation does not apply to debt servicing of school bonds approved by the voters and can also be exceeded by other taxing districts on voter approval. The city of Detroit also has a city charter rate limitation of 2 percent of assessed valuation for municipal taxation unless a specific increase is approved by the voters.[13]

The 1970 Tax Rates for Detroit

County	7.10
City	27.10
School	22.86

57.06 per $1,000 assessed valuation

Assessment targeted at 50 percent of actual value.

Nashville, Tennessee

The Tax.[14] The property tax in Tennessee is based upon county administration, but charter cities are also empowered to assess and collect their own taxes. There are in all ninety-five primary assessing areas in the state. The tax rate is the sum of county, municipal, school, and special district rates. The state receives no property-tax revenues.

Property Subject to Tax. All real and personal property not specifically exempted is subject to taxation. The principal exemption is a $1,000 personal property credit for each resident taxpayer. This exemption takes on added importance when a recent General Assembly law is noted: "Personal property ... used in the taxpayer's own household together with all intangible property including bank accounts of the taxpayer may be assumed prima facie by the tax assessor to be of a value not in excess of $1,000 in the absence of any tax return or schedule to the contrary."[15] This law flies in the face of a constitutional requirement of equality and uniformity of tax valuation throughout the state and has the effect of making only business property subject to personal tax. It has not been tested in court.

Assessment. Property is assessed at its fair market value. This assessment occurs annually for personal property and biennially in the odd years for real property for which a value of 50 percent will be required in 1973. This is to be attained by conforming to the following schedule: 1969, no less than 25 percent; 1970, 30 percent; 1971, 35 percent; 1972, 40 percent. Both federal and state courts have recently made rulings that should hasten Tennessee toward uniform assessment.[16]

The county or city assessor requires property owners to list their property. Assessments may be appealed to the County Board of Equalization or the Board of City Tax Equalization. Further appeal may be made to the State Board of Equalization, which has the power to increase or decrease valuations.[16] The "...same [valuation] may be revised or changed by the State Board of Equalization."[17]

Restrictions on Tax Power. The counties in Tennessee are subject to no general statutory rate limitations.on their property taxing power. Cities on the other hand are. The specific maximum rate for ordinary tax purposes in Nashville is 1.3 percent of assessed value. This does not include debt servicing but it still may act as a significant constraint as any increase beyond this requires a change in the city charter. Nashville is a nonhome rule charter city so the change must be made by the State General Assembly.

1970 Tax Rates for Nashville

	Rate per $1,000 assessed value
County	$35.00 (40 percent assessed to actual value)
City	$18.00 (40 percent assessed to actual value)
	$53.00

Oklahoma City, Oklahoma

The Tax.[18] Each of Oklahoma's seventy-seven counties is an administrative unit in the assessment and collection of taxes. An amendment to the constitution in 1933 abolished the state levy and established a primary levy limit of fifteen mills (exclusive of debt service) to be apportioned among the county, schools, and municipalities by the county excise board. This makes the cities largely dependent upon the counties for general revenue. Incorporated cities may, however, levy additional general property taxes on elected approval by vote of their citizens.

Property Subject to Tax. All property in the state is subject to ad valorem taxation unless exempt. Primary exemptions are: (1) homesteads up to $1,000 of assessed value, (2) family household goods up to $100, and (3) personal property of veterans or their widows up to $200. Neither the legislature nor cities can exempt any property not authorized by the constitution.

Assessment. Property is taxed at not to exceed 35 percent of its fair cash value. Uniformity of taxation within a city is required. Although the constitutional standard requires a fair cash-value base, assessed valuations seldom exceed half of actual value. Assessment is made yearly by the elected county assessor and may be appealed to the County Board of Equalization. Further appeal on individual valuation may be made to the District Court.[19] As would be expected from its title, the County Board also equalizes valuation within the county. A State Board of Equalization is also provided for.

" . . . It shall be the duty of said State Board [of Equalization] to examine the various county assessments and to equalize, correct, and adjust the same as between counties by increasing or decreasing the aggregate assessed value of the property or any class thereof. . . ."[20]

Lists of taxable property are required to be filed annually with the county assessor.

Restrictions on Tax Power. All taxing units are subject to a tax rate limit of fifteen mills excluding debt service unless an increase is specifically voted by the eligible voters of that unit.

The 1970 Tax Rate for Oklahoma City

School	48.15
City	22.80
County	19.78
	90.73 per $1,000 of assessed value.

Assessment targeted at 25 percent of actual value.

Philadelphia, Pennsylvania

The Tax.[21] Each of Pennsylvania's sixty-seven counties is a tax-assessment administrative unit. Counties are broken down into eight classes according to population, with Philadelphia being the only first class county (city population over one million).[22] Different legislative provisions affect each county according to class. The state receives no revenue from the property tax. In Philadelphia the tax rate (which includes school district taxes) is set by the City Council.

Property Subject to Tax. All real and personal property is subject to tax unless exempt. A principal exemption is the machinery and tools used in manufacturing.

Assessment. The valuation concept for assessment is the actual value of the property. In determining actual value, the price at which a property would separately bona fide sell shall be considered but shall not be controlling. In Philadelphia the legal assessment ratio is 100 percent. In practice this is not observed as evidenced by the determination of the State Tax Equalization Board for purposes of school subsidies in 1969 that the percentage of assessed valuation to market value in Philadelphia was 69.1 percent. In 4th to 8th class counties, real property must be assessed at a predetermined ratio not to exceed 75 percent. Although some assessors in the state are elected, assessors in Philadelphia are appointed by the Board of Revision of Taxes. Members of this board are appointed by a majority of the judges of the courts of common pleas. The Board of Revision of Taxes hears appeals and makes an annual equalization among all the properties.

Restrictions on Tax Power. The power granted to the city of Philadelphia to levy local taxes is subject to only one limitation—preemption of the tax by the state.[23] Other counties and municipalities of different classes are subject to various statutory tax limitations depending on class size.

1970 Property Tax Rate for Philadelphia

$44.75 per $1,000 assessed valuation

Assessment targeted at 65 percent of actual value.

Portland, Oregon

The Tax.[24] The thirty-six counties of Oregon are the base units for both property-tax assessment and collection. The rate in each county is the aggregate of all levies for state, county, municipal, and other special districts.

Property Subject to Tax. All real and tangible personal property is subject to tax unless exempt.[25] A principal exemption is nonbusiness tangible personal property. The personal residence of elderly people is also exempt a percentage of the first $10,000 valuation depending on age.

Assessment. Statutes require that all property be assessed at 100 percent of true cash value. Assessment valuations made by the county assessors are equalized on a local level by county boards of equalization. All values are then subject to final adjustment by the Department of Revenue sitting as a State Board of Equalization. Oregon takes a strong view toward tax uniformity throughout the state and the Department of Revenue exercises close supervisory power over the counties. "The Department of Revenue shall exercise general supervision of the system of taxation throughout the state, and general supervision and control over the administration of the assessment and tax laws and over county assessors and county boards of equalization in the performance of their duties relating to taxation to the end that all taxable property is assessed uniformly according to law and equality of taxation according to law is secured."[26] In all cases Department of Revenue directives may be appealed to the Oregon Tax Court.[27]

Although county assessors are elected, they must be certified and a law requires prosecution of any county assessor whose assessment ratio varies 20 percent or more from that determined by the department. Uniformity among counties is especially important because a large portion of the state revenues are derived from the property tax. Equalization on a statewide basis is required annually. The law also requires an annual return of personal property of all taxpayers.

Restrictions on Tax Power. A constitutional provision limits each local taxing unit's levies to 1.6 percent of the dollar amount levied in the highest of the preceding three years, exclusive of levies specifically authorized by the legislature or approved by local voter.[28] This limitation does not, however, apply to debt service.

The 1970-71 Tax Rate for Portland

$29.56 per $1,000 assessed valuation.

Assessment targeted at 100 percent of actual value

Providence, Rhode Island

The Tax.[29] Rhode Island follows the typical New England system in making the cities and towns rather than counties the units for local tax administration and in making the levy for state purposes in effect a levy against the respective cities and towns for their portions thereof, rather than a levy directly against the property of the taxpayers. Consequently, tax administration is dependent to a considerable extent on local administrative practice in the thirty-nine primary assessing areas.

Property Subject to Tax. All real and tangible personal property is subject to tax unless exempt. No city or town may assess any tax on intangible personal property. Exemptions are few in number compared to most states, the primary ones being: (1) manufacturer's inventories and (2) $1,000-$3,000 homestead exemptions for senior citizens in some towns (not Providence). The cities and towns also have the power to extend ten-year tax exemptions to attract commercial enterprises.[30] Providence, however, is not one of the cities that has chosen to take advantage of this provision.

Assessment. Real and personal property is taxable at its full and fair cash value or at a uniform assessment thereof not to exceed 100 percent.

Assessors may be either elected or appointed. Appeals from the local boards of assessors are made in the superior courts. The Division of Local and

Metropolitan Government has the "power to equalize the valuation of the property in the several cities and towns in the state by adding to or deducting from the aggregate valuations of the property in the cities and towns such sums as will bring said valuations to the true and market value of the property."[31] It does not have any original assessment or appellate functions. The town assessors publish notices requiring all taxpayers to file an account of their ratable property.

Restrictions on Tax Power. There is a statutory limitation of 3.5 percent of assessed value on the taxing power of the cities and towns. This does not include debt servicing, but it does include school taxes as there are no independent school districts in Rhode Island. The city or town may levy taxes in excess of this limit only by petitioning and receiving permission from the state director of administration.

1970 Tax Rate for Providence

$43.00 per $1,000 assessed valuation.

While Providence has targeted assessment at 80 percent of actual value, the Division of Local and Metropolitan Government determined that in 1970 the ratio of assessment to full value was 65.76 percent.

San Francisco, California

The Tax.[32] The fifty-eight counties of California are the primary base units for the assessment and collection of property taxes. The rate is a composite of the state, county, municipal, school district, and special district levies. A state statute limits the amount of all state fund appropriations to be derived from property taxes to 25 percent of such appropriations.[33] Although the state has reserved the right to levy property taxes, it never has.

Property Subject to Tax. All real and tangible personal property is subject to tax unless exempt. Principal exemptions include: (1) a householder's exemption of $100, and (2) veteran's exemptions of $1,000, and if disabled or blind, to $5,000.

Assessment. All taxable property except aircraft is assessed at a publicly announced ratio of between 20 and 25 percent of full cash value, and beginning in 1971, at 25 percent of full cash value. This assessment is almost entirely in the hands of elected county assessors. The County Board of Supervisors hears appeals and is required to make an annual equalization of property valuation. This decision is final as to individual properties in the absence of any showing of fraud. At least once each three years, the State Board of Equalization conducts a survey to determine the full cash value of all locally assessable tangible property. The State Board may direct that the entire assessment roll of any county be increased or lowered, but it may not adjust or revise individual assessments. . . . "Equalization shall be by raising or lowering the value of locally assessable property entered upon the secured roll by the assessor of the county."[34]

Taxpayers owning taxable personal property of $30,000 or more are required to file an enumeration list of their property with the county assessor. He may also request a written property statement from other property owners if he so desires.

Restrictions on the Tax Power. There is no general limitation on counties, but county levies authorized for a few specific purposes may be subject to some rate limits. Municipalities, school districts, and special districts are subject to statutory rate limits that can be exceeded only by voter approval of the specific increase in the respective district. Debt servicing levies do not usually fall within the restrictions.

1970 Tax Rate for San Francisco

128.20 per $1,000 assessed valuation

Assessment/sales ratio 22 percent. Entire state moving toward target ratio of 25 percent.

Appendix: D
Investor Questionnaire

Interviewer _____

City _____

Respondent _____

Date _____

INTRODUCTORY TELEPHONE CALL

My name is _____ and I am part of a research team carrying out a study for the U.S. Department of Housing and Urban Development. The study is concerned with center city property owners and managers, and the problems they encounter in the ownership and maintenance of property in the city. We are especially interested in finding out what effect property taxation has on the maintenance and improvement of properties. We are talking to property owners and managers in ten cities all over the country. Your name has been given to us as an owner of property here in _____ , (*name city*). Can we make an appointment to talk with you? The terms of our contract with the Department of Housing and Urban Development provide that any information we receive during this study from particular property owners will be strictly confidential. No information will be given to either HUD or any other government agency or official in a form that will identify data with the participants in our study.

INTERVIEW

Repeat above introduction, say something about yourself here to make the atmosphere more informal if you choose. See interview instructions for possible introductory conversation.

1. Let's talk about the properties you own.
   a. How many properties and units do you own in all? (*Find out whether these are commercial or residential properties, and classify according to table below.*)

PROPERTY DATA SHEET

Commercial	Residential	
	1-29 Units	30+ Units

   b. How do land and property values in the neighborhood where the property(ies) under consideration is (are) located compare with values in this city generally? (*See definitions–Operational Selection of Neighborhood. Note respondent's definition of his neighborhood boundaries and note how it compares with the neighborhood boundary we have developed through city reconnaissance. Obtain data from Assessor's records whenever possible.*)

	Property 1			Property 2			Property 3		
	Above Aver.	Below Aver.	Aver.	Above Aver.	Below Aver.	Aver.	Above Aver.	Below Aver.	Aver.
Current Land Values									
Current Value of Buildings or Improvements									
Current Total Property Value									

c. Have prices in this neighborhood increased, decreased or stayed the same since 1966? Why? (*See definitions–Operational Selection of Neighborhood.*)

	Property 1			Property 2			Property 3		
	Up	Down	Same	Up	Down	Same	Up	Down	Same
Current Land Values as compared to those of 1966									
Current Value of Buildings or Improvements as compared to those of 1966									
Current Total Property Values as compared to those of 1966									

d. Have prices in this neighborhood increased or decreased relatively more or less than in the city generally since 1966 (e.g., was there a larger percentage change in prices)? (*See definitions—Operational Selection of Neighborhood.*)

	Property 1			Property 2			Property 3		
	Above Aver.	Below Aver.	Aver.	Above Aver.	Below Aver.	Aver.	Above Aver.	Below Aver.	Aver.
Increased: Land Values									
Value of Buildings or Improvements									
Total Property Values									
Decreased: Land Values									
Value of Buildings or Improvements									
Total Property Values									

e. (*Interviewer, classify neighborhood(s) on basis of definitions of neighborhoods.*)

	Stable	Trans.↑	Trans.↓	Blighted
Property 1				
Property 2				
Property 3				

f. Do you regard the public services such as schools, libraries, public transportation, neighborhood centers adequate to serve the needs of the neighborhood? Why?

2. a. Why did you acquire this property? (More than one box may be checked for each property? for instance a *short term* investment may reflect *cash flow* considerations.)

	Property 1	Property 2	Property 3
Inherited			
Cash flow			
Tax shelter			
Long term investment			
Short term investment			
Other *(specify)*			

b. How long do you intend to keep it (from date initially acquired)?

	Property 1	Property 2	Property 3
No. years intend to keep			

c. *Summarize his investment strategy according to categories below and confirm, e.g., "then you are in the habit of investing for long-term?". If investor mentions more than one investment strategy, rank them in order (e.g., 1,2). See definitions of long-term and short-term.*

Investment Strategy	Rank
Long-term capital appreciation	
Long-term rental income	
Short-term capital appreciation	
Short-term rental income (cash flow)	
Tax shelter	
Other (specify)	

3. *Identify the property(ies).* How would you describe each of your properties? *According to your matrix, get answers to fill in data sheet below and write others in space provided. (Compare the investor's classification of neighborhoods with the assessor's and other informants' descriptions of price movements which provide the basis for neighborhood classification.)*

	Property 1	Property 2	Property 3
Address			
Investor Report			
Neighborhood (stable, trans. ↑ ↓ , blighted)			
Assessor Report			
Neighborhood (stable trans. ↑ ↓ , blighted)			
*Age of building (no. of yrs. old)			
*Number of previous owners			
Number of dwelling units			
Purchased (P) or inherited (I)			
Year P or I			
Live in building?			
Commercial (C)/Residential (R)			

Obtain this information from Assessor's records or other public records whenever possible.

4. Are you the sole owner of this property or do you own it in a partnership, a real estate investment trust, a corporation, or another arrangement?

	Property 1	Property 2	Property 3
Sole owner			
Partnership			
Corporation			
Real estate investment trust			
Other *(specify)*			

4a. *If other than sole owner:* Who makes the decisions regarding the management of this property?

	Property 1	Property 2	Property 3
I do			
Someone else or joint *(specify)*			

5. Let's talk specifically about the neighborhood. Has the ethnic mix changed since 1966? (*See definitions—Operational Selection of Neighborhood*)

	Property 1		Property 2		Property 3	
	1966	1971	1966	1971	1966	1971
Neighborhood % Black (B) % White (W); % Other *(specify)*						

6. a. Now, about your tenants, what is the racial composition and household income of the tenants at this property(ies)?

Race:	Property 1	Property 2	Property 3
% Black			
% White			
% Other *(specify)*			

Household Income:	Property 1	Property 2	Property 3
Below $3K/year			
$3– 5K			
$5–10K			
Over $10K			

   b. Have tenants become more insistent on repairs and unkeep? (*Check data box below and jot down notes in space provided.*)

Tenant demands for repair and upkeep since 1966:	Property 1	Property 2	Property 3
Up			
Down			
Same			

c. Have the characteristics of your tenants changed since 1966? (*If yes, check the appropriate box(es).*)

	Property 1	Property 2	Property 3
Younger			
Older			
More students			
More retired			
More ADC (welfare)			
More Whites			
More Blacks			
More other minority groups			
More children			
Less income			
More income			

d. Average number of children per household

	Property 1	Property 2	Property 3

7. a. How many apartments are presently vacant in this building? Is this level materially different from what it was in 1966?

	Property 1	Property 2	Property 3
Number units vacant			
Current Vacancy Level Compared to that of 1966 Up			
Down			
Same			

b. Has the average period of vacancy changed since 1966?

	Property 1	Property 2	Property 3
Current Average Period of Vacancy Compared to that of 1966: Up			
Down			
Same			

c. What is the current average turnover for your tenants and how has it changed since 1966? (*Check data box below and make notes in space provided.*)

Turnover	Property 1	Property 2	Property 3
6 months or less			
1/2 year to one year			
1−2 years			
More than two years			
Change Up			
Down			
Same			

8. What do you think the current market value of this property is? On what basis do you make this estimate? If you were to sell your property today, would it market value have appreciated, depreciated, or remained the same since you purchased this property? (*See definitions–Calculation of Market Value of Properties (appreciation, depreciation)*.)

	Property 1	Property 2	Property 3
Current Market Value 　Land			
Buildings or Improvements			
Total			
How estimated (e.g., comparable properties, recent offers, other.)			
Appreciate (A), Depreciate (D) Remain the Same (S)			

9. a. What average rents do you charge monthly for:

	Property 1	Property 2	Property 3
Efficiency/studio			
One bedroom			
Two bedroom			
Three bedroom			
Commercial *(specify)*			

   b. What services does this include?

	Property 1	Property 2	Property 3
Heat			
Water			
Electricity			
Furnished			
Other *(specify)*			

10. Who does minor building maintenance? (*Check data box below and jot down notes in space provided.*)

Maintenance	Property 1	Property 2	Property 3
Janitor			
Superintendent			
Management firm			
Contract cleaner			
Other *(specify)*			

Now I would like to ask you about some of the costs involved in owning property.

11. a. What was the purchase price of the property?

	Property 1	Property 2	Property 3
Price ($)			
Year purchased			

b. What does your present debt structure look like? (*Check the data box below and note comments in space provided.*)

First Mortgage	Property 1	Property 2	Property 3
Purchase Money Mortgage			
Takeover or assumption of mortgage			
Type mortgage (e.g. conv., FHA VA)			
Interest rate			
Original maturity (years)			
Years remaining			
Principal remaining			

Second Mortgage	Property 1	Property 2	Property 3
Takeover or assumption			
Lender (e.g., seller; other indiv.; bank)			
Interest rate			
Original maturity			
Years remaining			
Principal remaining			

Other	Property 1	Property 2	Property 3
Takeover or assumption of mortgage			
Lender (e.g., seller; other indiv.; bank)			
Interest rate			
Original maturity			
Years remaining			
Principal remaining			

c. Were you concerned about rises in the property tax when you purchased the property? If so, what was the nature of your concern?

12. Now let's talk about your gross income and expenditures from this building. (*Ask about gross income and percent change since 1966; costs for each year since 1966 and percentage change in costs since 1966. Check data boxes and note comments in space provided.*)

a. Gross Income
Each Year Since 1966

1966			
1967			
1968			
1969			
1970			

	Property 1	Property 2	Property 3
% change in gross income since 1966			

b. Costs (in dollars)
Each Year Since 1966

Property 1	1966	1967	1968	1969	1970
Administration/management					
Insurance					
Utilities					
Maintenance					
Debt Service					
Property taxes					
Other taxes					
Reserve for replacements or extraordinary repairs					
Other expenses					
Total expenses					

Costs (in dollars)
Each Year Since 1966

Property 2

	1966	1967	1968	1969	1970
Administration/management					
Insurance					
Utilities					
Maintenance					
Debt Service					
Property taxes					
Other taxes					
Reserve for replacements or extraordinary repairs					
Other expenses					
Total expenses					

Costs (in dollars)
Each Year Since 1966

Property 3

	1966	1967	1968	1969	1970
Administration/management					
Insurance					
Utilities					
Maintenance					
Debt Service					
Property taxes					
Other taxes					
Reserve for replacements or extraordinary repairs					
Other expenses					
Total expenses					

12. c. Could you summarize, then, how your cash flow has changed since 1966?

13. Property taxes represent _____ percent of the market value of this property? (*Take market value from question 8, property tax from question 12, calculate effective tax rate, and check this with investor—Obtain this information from Assessor's records whenever possible.*)

	Property 1	Property 2	Property 3
Effective Tax Rate (per ADL calculation)	%	%	%
Effective Tax Rate (Assessors Record)	%	%	%

14. (*Check Assessor's records for data on the effective tax rate in the neighbor-hoods where these properties are located.*)

	Property 1	Property 2	Property 3
Average Neighborhood Effective Tax Rate			

15. a. If your taxes are increased, do you pass the increase on to the tenants?

	Property 1	Property 2	Property 3
Tax Passed on			
How soon after tax increase			
Tax not passed on			

  b. (*Interviewer: calculate what percentage of gross income goes toward property taxes by comparing answers to Question 12a and 12b.*)

	Property 1	Property 2	Property 3
% gross income			

  c. (*If assessment records do not reveal the information.*) At what point, in relation to the due date, do you pay your property taxes?

	Property 1	Property 2	Property 3
Less than 1 month before due			
1 to 3 months before due			
More than 3 months before due			
After they are due			

  d. If after, why?

16. Thinking in terms of maintenance repairs and rehabilitation, how frequently do you: (*ask each category, but don't read the intervals.*)

PROPERTY 1	At Regular Intervals *(state interval)*	At Tenant Request	At Apt. Turnover	When Necessary	Other *(specify)*
Window cleaning					
General cleaning					
Trash removal					
Lighting					
Minor plumbing					
Minor electrical repair					
Paint job Apartments					
Common area					
Exterior					
Decorating					
New bathroom appliances					
New kitchen appliances					

PROPERTY 2	At Regular Intervals *(state interval)*	At Tenant Request	At Apt. Turnover	When Necessary	Other *(specify)*
Window cleaning					
General cleaning					
Trash removal					
Lighting					
Minor plumbing					
Minor electrical repair					
Paint job Apartments					
Common area					
Exterior					
Decorating					
New bathroom appliances					
New kitchen appliances					

PROPERTY 3	At Regular Intervals *(state interval)*	At Tenant Request	At Apt. Turnover	When Necessary	Other *(specify)*
Window cleaning					
General cleaning					
Trash removal					
Lighting					
Minor plumbing					
Minor electrical repair					
Paint job Apartments					
Common area					
Exterior					
Decorating					
New bathroom appliances					
New kitchen appliances					

17. a. Since 1966, have you done any of the following rehabilitation in any of these buildings?

	Property 1				Property 2				Property 3			
	No	Yes	Year	Cost	No	Yes	Year	Cost	No	Yes	Year	Cost
a. Heating Plant												
b. rewiring												
c. new lobby												
d. plumbing												
e. changing apartment size												
f. replastering												
g. external improvements												

skip to Q23   skip to Q23   skip to Q23

b. What was the major reason behind each of these improvements?
(*Commercial: only for those expenditures paid by owner—note rehabilitation type for each—See definitions of rehab. Note: Do not read alternatives*)

	Property 1	Property 2	Property 3
Replacement of worn-out equipment			
Pride of ownership			
To get new tenants			
To keep tenants			
Code violations			
Other (specify)			

18. Was it necessary to obtain a building permit for each of these changes? (*Specify type of rehab*)

Building Permit	Property 1—Rehab Episode			
	I	II	III	IV
Yes				
No				

	Property 2—Rehab Episode			
	I	II	III	IV
Yes.				
No				

	Property 3—Rehab Episode			
	I	II	III	IV
Yes				
No				

19. Generally, what kinds of improvements that a property owner makes to his property are likely to result in an increased assessment?

	Yes	No
Any improvement requiring a building permit		
Any exterior improvement		
Any time you purchase a new property, the property is reassessed		
Any improvement which eliminates a code violation		

Now I'd like to ask a bit about the consequence of your rehabilitation.

20. a. Were you reassessed as a direct result of the rehabilitation which you told me about? (*See definitions of rehab. Specify type of rehabilitation.*) What was your assessment rate before rehabilitation? What was it after?

	Property 1 Rehab Episode				Property 2 Rehab Episode				Property 3 Rehab Episode			
	I	II	III	IV	I	II	III	IV	I	II	III	IV
Type of rehab												
Reassessed Yes												
No												
*Assessment values ($) Before												
After												
*Property Tax Before												
After												

Obtain information from Assessor's records or other public records whenever possible.

b. How soon after the rehab were you reassessed?

	Property 1 Rehab Episode				Property 2 Rehab Episode				Property 3 Rehab Episode			
	I	II	III	IV	I	II	III	IV	I	II	III	IV
Date of rehab												
Date of reassessment												

c. What was your reaction to reassessment?

d. In each case, how did the change in the assessment compare with the cost of the improvement(s)?

	Property 1 Rehab Episode				Property 2 Rehab Episode				Property 3 Rehab Episode			
	I	II	III	IV	I	II	III	IV	I	II	III	IV
Change in assessment												
Cost of improvements												

21. What about financing? Did you get financing for the rehab work? What type of financing did you use? What percentage of the work was financed? (*Specify type of rehabilitation*)

Property 1	Not Financed	Personal Loan	Mortgage	Other	% Financed	Interest Rate
Rehab I:						
Rehab II:						
Rehab III:						
Rehab IV:						

Property 2	Not Financed	Personal Loan	Mortgage	Other	% Financed	Interest Rate
Rehab I:						
Rehab II:						
Rehab III:						
Rehab IV:						

Property 3	Not Financed	Personal Loan	Mortgage	Other	% Financed	Interest Rate
Rehab I:						
Rehab II:						
Rehab III:						
Rehab IV:						

22. a. After you rehabbed, did you find it necessary to raise rents. If so, by how much?

	Property 1 Rehab Episode				Property 2 Rehab Episode				Property 3 Rehab Episode			
	I	II	III	IV	I	II	III	IV	I	II	III	IV
Rent raised yes												
no-*skip to Q22b*												
How long after rehab?												
How much?												
Year before cover cost (e.g., number of years to recoup cost)												

b. Did the number of vacancies change as a result of this rehabilitation? (*Note rehabilitation type for each*)

	Property 1 Rehab Episode				Property 2 Rehab Episode				Property 3 Rehab Episode			
	I	II	III	IV	I	II	III	IV	I	II	III	IV
No												
Yes number before rehabilitation												
number after rehabilitation												

c. From your experience, are properties which are kept in POOR condition assessed LOWER in relation to actual market value than properties kept in GOOD condition?

Higher _____   Same _____

Lower _____   Don't know _____

d. Do you think this situation contributes to neighborhood blight or improvement? Why?

23. a. (*Nonrehabilitators only*) Have you ever considered rehabilitating?

	Property 1	Property 2	Property 3
No–*skip to Q23c*			
Yes			

b. *If yes*, What are you considering doing in the next two years? (*Jot notes in space provided*)

What Planned?	A Htg	B Wiring	C Plumbg	D Partit	E Plast	F Adds	G Ext	H Other
Property 1								
Property 2								
Property 3								

c. *If not*, Why not?

difficult to obtain financing								
fear of reassessment								
deterioration of neighborhood								
unavailability of labor								
other								
rents could not be raised to cover costs								

24. a. (*Ask both rehabilitators and nonrehabilitators*). In your case, what are the most significant obstacles to rehabilitation? Rank the following from 0 to 5, with 0 the least and 5 the most significant obstacles.

	Rank
Difficulty of obtaining financing	_____
Fear of reassessment	_____
Deterioration of neighborhood	_____
Unavailability of labor	_____
other	_____

b. What factors might induce you to undertake needed rehabilitation or repairs? (If rehabilitation has already been undertaken, what factors might have induced you to undertake it sooner or more intensively?)

c. If you had a five-year abatement from reassessment due to major rehabilitation, would this affect your plans for rehabilitation?

Yes _____ No _____

d. Would your reaction be any different if you were to receive a credit against the property tax owed in the year of rehab, instead of a five-year abatement from reassessment?

Yes _____ No _____

e. How much of a tax credit would you deem necessary to induce major rehab?

f. (*If a willingness to rehabilitate is indicated*).

	Property 1	Property 2	Property 3
What rehabilitation would you do?			

25. How has the assessed value of each of these properties changed since 1966? (*Obtain this information from Assessor's records or other public records whenever possible.*) Why?

	Property 1	Property 2	Property 3
Assessed valuation at date of purchase			
Year assessment changed			
Why?			
rehabilitation			
town assessment			
random assessment			
don't know			
other *(specify)*			
Current assessed valuation			

26. a. Have you ever appealed the assessment of your property?

Yes _____ No _____

If yes, what were the results?	Property 1	Property 2	Property 3
No change			
Assessment decreased less than 10%			
Assessment decreased more than 10%			

    b. Are you concerned about possible increases in the property tax? Why?

    c. Are assessments made equitably throughout the city?

27. What do you think keeps some people from maintaining and upgrading their property? (*Do not read alternatives.*)

	Yes	No
Properties rehabilitated will get increased assessment		
Building permit = tax increase		
External improvements will bring in assessor		
Assessors redo whole property, not just changes		
New property owner always reassessed		
Difficulty of obtaining financing		
Fear of reassessment		
Deterioration of neighborhood		
Unavailability of labor		
Other *(specify)*		

28. What specific changes, if any, in the property tax and its administration would you recommend to encourage more landlords to keep their property in good repair? (*Jot notes in space below. Builders: ask specifically incentives needed for new construction; effect of differential tax or reassessment on new construction. Ask how the tax rate compares with other surrounding areas and its impact on rehabilitation and new development decisions.*)

29. Could you comment on the following alternates which have been suggested as possible means of reform? Comment on each alternative using the terms "very desirable", "desirable", "undesirable" and "very undesirable". Then rank the best three alternatives 1-2-3 in the order of your preference.

	Comment	Rank

Alternative 1:
Assessing property on the basis of present use of land without regard to improvements or physical deterioration?   _____   _____

Alternative 2:
Assessing property on the basis of the highest and best use of land only, without regard to improvements or physical deterioration or present zoning;   _____   _____

Alternative 3:
Assessing property so that land values are subject to a higher rate than improvements;   _____   _____

Alternative 4:
Assessing income-producing property on the basis of capitalization of net income (rental receipts minus expenses for operations, maintenance, repairs and replacement);   _____   _____

Alternative 5:
Assessing income-producing property on the basis of a fixed proportion (e.g., 15 percent) of annual gross rent receipts;   _____   _____

Alternative 6:
Reassessing property improvements, but offering a five-year tax abatement on the improvement;   _____   _____

Alternative 7:
Imposing higher taxes on properties in violation of local housing and building codes;   _____   _____

Alternative 8:
Assess properties on the basis of their present use, but assume standard conditions, e.g., full compliance with the local codes. (This approach involves a penalty for properties which are kept in substandard condition.)   _____   _____

Alternative 9:
Assess properties on the basis of the current method of assessment.   _____   _____

Thank respondent and terminate.

Appendix: E
Property Data Sheet

(Using data from official records, complete one copy of this form for each property included in the survey.)

Address of property:

Owner:

Date(s) data were assembled

Sources:

I. General Background

   1. Year Built:

   2. Dates and sales prices of transfers:

Dates	Initial Acq.									
Prices										

   3. Assessment history:

Dates Assessed										
Value Assigned										
Land Only										

4. Property tax history over the last ten years:

	Assessed Value	Rate	Amount of tax	Paid on time? "yes" "no" If no, date paid	Appeal filed Date action
1961					
1962					
1963					
1964					
1965					
1966					
1967					
1968					
1969					
1970					

II. Questions included on Investor and/or Homeowner Questionnaires for which data should be obtained initially from Assessor's records or other public records (includes questions not covered above).

1. How do current total property values (land and improvements) in the neighborhood compare to those of 1966?

Up	Down	Same

2. How do changes in total property values in this neighborhood compare to price movements in the city, generally?

Above Average	Average Change	Below Average

Notes

Notes

Chapter 1
Introduction

1. Charles F. Bastable, *Public Finance* (London: MacMillan, 1892), p. 424.

2. E.R.A. Seligman, *Essays in Taxation* (New York: Macmillan, 1903), p. 47.

3. Dick Netzer, *Impact of the Property Tax: Its Economic Implication for Urban Problems*, Prepared for the National Commission on Urban Problems (Washington, D.C., U.S. Government Printing Office, 1968), p. 9.

4. George Stenlieb, *The Tenement Landlord* (New Brunswick, N.J.: Urban Studies Center, 1966).

Chapter 2
The Property Tax and Neighborhood Analysis

1. For an interesting analysis of a noneconomic response to business adversity, see Albert O. Hirschman, *Exit, Voice and Loyalty* (Cambridge, Mass.: Harvard University Press, 1972). Hirschman, an economist, argues that economists have been lax in failing to recognize the important patterns of corporate response to adverse economic situations.

2. George Akahoshi and Edna Gass, *A Study of the Problems of Abandoned Housing and Recommendations for Action by the Federal Government and Localities*, Washington: Linton, Mields and Costen, 1971. This study was commissioned by the U.S. Department of Housing and Urban Development. For other similar approaches see National Urban League and the Center for Community Change, *The National Survey of Housing Abandonment*, New York, 1971, and the Institute for Urban and Regional Studies, *Urban Decay in St. Louis* (St. Louis, Missouri: Washington University, March 1972).

3. George Sternlieb and Robert W. Burchell *Residential Abandonment: The Tenement Landlord Revisited*. Center for Urban Policy Research, Rutgers University, New Brunswick, New Jersey, July 1972 (mimeo). This study is scheduled to be published in revised form by Transaction Press, New Brunswick, New Jersey.

4. For a rigorous analysis of the effect of general property taxes on the gross and net return to capital under varying market conditions see Peter Mieszkowski, "The Property Tax: An Excise Tax or a Property Tax," *Cowles Foundation*, Discussion Paper No. 304, Yale University, New Haven, Conn., November 1970. Also, see Ronald E. Grieson, "The Economics of Property Taxes and Land Values," Department of Economics Working Paper No. 72, Massachusetts Institute of Technology, Cambridge, Mass., June 1971.

Chapter 3
Variation in Property-Tax Rates

1. For a summary of the disincentive arguments, see Dick Netzer, *Economics of the Property Tax* (Washington, D.C.: The Brookings Institute, 1966).

2. The legal interpretation of "market value" or "true cash value" varies from state to state. Most cities are not obliged to accept actual sales as determinative of market value. They may also adduce comparable sales, the capitalized value of a property's income stream and reproduction costs minus depreciation and obsolescence as basis for estimating market value. However, all cities agree that assessment/market sales ratios represent the best check on the accuracy of assessment. See Assessor Interview question 4.

3. See, for example, John Lansing and Leslie Kish, "Response Error in Estimating the Value of Housing," *Journal of American Statistical Association* 49 (September 1954), pp. 520-538. For a study using more recent data, see John F. Kain and John M. Quigley, "Measuring the Quality and Cost of Housing," *Journal of the American Statistical Association* 65 (June 1970), pp. 532-48.

4. For evidence drawn from a much larger data base on neighborhood variation in assessment sales ratios for Boston, see Oliver Oldman and Henry Aaron, "Assessment Sales Ratios Under the Boston Property Tax," *National Tax Journal* 17 (March 1966).

5. The implications of neighborhood variations in gross-rent multipliers for the regressivity or progressivity of property taxation is developed more formally by George E. Peterson, "The Regressivity of Residential Property Taxation," *Journal of Public Economics*, forthcoming.

6. Netzer, *Economics of the Property Tax.*

Chapter 4
Blighted Neighborhoods

1. While much has been written on the crisis ghetto, the work of George Sternlieb and the Rutgers University Center for Urban Policy Research deserves special mention. Of particular interest is George Sternlieb and Robert W. Burchell, *Residential Abandonment: The Tenement Landlord Revisited* (New Brunswick, N.J. Transaction Press, forthcoming). This study had the advantage of following up the previous work of Sternlieb reported in *The Tenement Landlord* (New Brunswick, N.J.: Urban Studies Center, 1966). The authors were able to analyze changes in the attitudes of landlords and the characteristics of structures over a seven-year period. For an interesting article which focuses on the racial aspects of the housing management problem, see Franklin J. James, "Race and Profit and Housing Abandonment in Newark," a paper presented at the Joint Meetings of the American Economics and American Real Estate and Urban Economics Associations, Toronto, Canada, December 1972.

2. For an interesting survey of the variation in the supply costs of housing across spatially separated neighborhood submarkets, see Robert Schafer et al., *The Spatial Variation in Housing Costs*. Department of City and Regional Planning, Harvard University, Cambridge, Mass., February 1973 (mimeo).

3. For a formal statement of this proposition as well as an interesting discussion of the abandonment process, see Gregory K. Ingram and John F. Kain, "Simple Analytics of Housing Abandonment," a paper presented at the meetings of the American Economics and American Real Estate and Urban Economics Associations, Toronto, Ontario, Canada, December 1972.

4. As an illustration of the decline in maintenance expenditures that can result from the application of rent control see John C. Morehouse, "Optimal Housing Maintenance Under Rent Control," *Southern Economic Journal*, Vol. XXXIX, No. 1 (July 1972), pp. 93-107.

5. For an interesting discussion of the dynamics of decline see William Grigsby, et al., *Housing and Poverty*, Institute for Environmental Studies, University of Pennsylvania, April 1971 (mimeo). Also, see Phillip H. Friedly, "Experimental Approaches to the Amelioration of Housing Abandonment and Neighborhood Decline," paper presented at the annual meetings of the American Real Estate and Urban Economics Association, New Orleans, December 1971.

6. William Lilley III and Timothy B. Clark, "Federal Programs Spur Abandonment of Housing in Major Cities," *National Journal*, January 1, 1972, pp. 26-33.

7. Similar conclusions were reached by James in his "Race and Profit." James observed that white owners with black tenants were more likely to abandon properties than black owners with black tenants, and otherwise similar circumstances.

8. See Michael A. Stegman, *Housing Investment in the Inner City* (Cambridge: M.I.T. Press, 1972) and George Sternlieb and Robert Burchell, *Residential Abandonment: The Tenement Landlord Revisited*, op. cit.

9. Additional information on the lack of concentration of ownership can be found in Michael A. Stegman, *Housing Investment in the Innner City*, op. cit.

Chapter 5
Downward Transitional Neighborhoods

1. The 1960 and 1970 data is taken from the U.S. Bureau of the Census, Census of Population and Housing, *Detailed Housing Characteristics, United States Summary*.

2. This has been the reasoning behind a variety of federal programs. See, for example, Jonathan Spivak, "Pride of Ownership: Government is Testing a Plan to Help the Poor Buy Their Own Homes," *Wall Street Journal*, October 23, 1970. For a more ambitious proposal see Sheldon Schreiberg, "Abandoned

Buildings: Tenant Condominiums and Community Redevelopment," *Urban Lawyer*, Vol. 2, Spring 1970, pp. 186-218.

Chapter 6
The Property Tax and Federally
Subsidized Housing

1. The section 236 and 221(d)(3) programs refer to FHA mortgage-insured rental projects in which the government lowers tenant rental payments by assuming a portion of the monthly interest payment on the mortgage.

2. For a general discussion of the risks involved in central-city investments, see Michael A. Stegman, *Housing Investment in the Inner City*, op. cit.

3. This is the same formula used throughout the country by local housing authorities. For both conventional and turnkey public housing, the LHA pays the municipal government 10 percent of shelter rents (gross rents minus utilities) in lieu of full tax payments.

4. For an analysis of the net impact of various federally-subsidized housing projects on local tax revenues, see Arthur P. Solomon, *Housing the Urban Poor: An Analysis of Federal Housing Policy* (Cambridge: M.I.T. Press, forthcoming).

Chapter 8
Stable Neighborhoods

1. For good summaries of this literature, see David Bradford and Wallace Oates, "The Suburban Exploitation Thesis," in Harold M. Hochman and George E. Peterson, ed., *Redistribution and Public Choice* (Columbia University Press: 1973) and William B. Neenan, *Political Economy of Urban Areas* (Markham: 1972).

2. Data for Baltimore are taken from William H. Oakland, "Financing Urban Government: The Case of Baltimore," paper delivered at the Committee for Urban Economy Conference, January 12-13, 1973.

3. See, for example, George E. Peterson and Arthur P. Solomon, "Property Taxes and Populist Reform," *The Public Interest* (Winter 1973).

Chapter 9
Implementing the Property-Tax System

1. While still in the formative stage, the use of computers to appraise the value of individual properties is beginning to catch on in an increasing number of cities. For a description of the application of computerized techniques in the

appraisal process see Jack Lessinger, "Econometrics and Appraisal," *The Appraisal Journal* (1969) 37, no. 4; Andrew J. Hinshaw, "The Assessor and the Computerization of Data," *The Appraisal Journal* (1969) 37, no. 2.; and Theodore R. Smith "Multiple Regression and the Appraisal of Single Family Residential Properties," *Appraisal Journal* (April 1971) 39, no. 2.

2. Other studies on appeals procedures include Myron H. Ross, "The Property Tax Assessment Review Process: A Cause of Regressive Property Taxation?" *National Tax Journal* (March 1971), pp. 32-43; Richard N. Rossett, "Inequity in the Real Property Tax of New York State and the Aggravating Effect of Litigation," *National Tax Journal* (March 1970), pp. 66-73. These and other studies indicate that formal appeals do little to increase the overall equity of assessments.

Chapter 10
Property-Tax Alternatives

1. For a detailed study of the achievements of tax abatement and other incentive policies, see Price Waterhouse and Co., *A Study of the Effects of Real Estate Property Tax Incentive Programs Upon Property Rehabilitation and New Construction*. Report to the U.S. Department of Housing and Urban Development (February 1973).

Appendix C
City-State Property-Tax Statutes

1. Georgia Code, 1933—Chap. 92-1, 92-2, 92-23, 92-24, 92-26 to 92-28, 92-37 to 92-83, and 32-11.

2. Annotated Code of Maryland, 1957, Article 81; Baltimore Charter.

3. Annotated Code Art. 81, Sec. 258.

4. Chapter 757, Acts of 1959; Ch. 9, Laws 1961.

5. Baltimore Charter, Art. II, Sec. 40.

6. Revenue Act of 1939, I.

7. III Const. Art. IX, Sec. 1.

8. See Irving Howard, "Property Tax Rate Limits in Illinois and Their Effect Upon Local Government," *National Tax Journal* 16 (September 1963), pp. 285-93.

9. Compiled Laws 1948, Chapter 211.

10. Mich. Const. Article 9, Sec. 3; Laws 1965, Act 409.

11. Compiled Laws, Sec. 211.152.

12. Compiled Laws, Sec. 211.34.

13. Charter of the City of Detroit, Title VI, Ch. I, Sec. 1.

14. Tennessee Code, Title 67; Ch. 1-21.

15. Tennessee, *Public Acts* (1959), Ch. 279, Sec. 4, pp. 874-75.

16. Louisville and N.R.R. vs Public Service Commission, 249 F. Supp 894 (1966), Southern Ry vs Clement, Davidson County Chancevy Court II, Book 77 (1966), p. 191.

17. T.C.A., Sec. 67-809.

18. Oklahoma Statutes, Title 68, Article 24.

19. O.S. Tit. 68, Sec. 2461.

20. O.S. Tit. 68, Sec. 2463.

21. Public Law 45, Act of Aug. 5, 1932.

22. Public Law 275, Act of June 25, 1895.

23. Public Law 45, Act of Aug. 5, 1932, Sec. 1.

24. Oregon Revised Statutes, Title 29, Chapters 306-12.

25. O.R.S., 307.030.

26. O.R.S., 305.090.

27. O.R.S., 306.545.

28. Const. of Oregon, Art. XI, Sec. 11.

29. The Laws, Title 28, Ch. 17; Tit. 44, Ch. 1,3-8,9,25; Title 45 Ch. 12.

30. General Laws (1956), Sec. 44-3-9.

31. General Laws, Sec. 42-11, 1-2.

32. Revenue and Taxation Code, Division 1.

33. Revenue and Taxation Code, Section 1605; Eastern-Columbia Inc. County of Los Angeles et al. (1945), 70 Cal. App. 2d 497, 161 P 2d 407.

34. Revenue and Taxation Code, Sec. 1821.

Index

Abandonment: causes of, 11-12; premature, 43; process of, 41, 44, 116
Abatement policy, 88, 109-110, 113-114; granting, 116
Absentee landlords and owners, 7, 40, 61, 63-64
Accomodations, quality of, 13
Administration: problems of, 97, 113, 116; of property tax, 6
Advisory Commission on Intergovernmental Relations, 93
Age; housing stock, 26-29, 59, 105; neighborhood, 67; population, 90
Aid, state, 92
Akahoshi, George, cited, 12-13
American Economic Association, 1
Amortization, payments on, 13
Apartments, luxury, 99
Appeals procedure, 52-53, 74, 97, 106-107, 121; in Baltimore, 107
Appraising and appraisers, 105
Appreciation, capital, 82
Assessment: appeals, 52; of improvements, 86; local, 102; mass computerized programs, 121; negative, 102; objection of, 108; in Portland, 99; practices and methods, 7-8, 69, 72, 97-100; reduction in, 107; reforms, 57
Assessment sales ratios, 19, 21, 97-99, 102-105, 108, 121
Assessors, local, 4, 73, 104
Atlanta, Georgia: fire protection zone, 91; statues, 139-140; summary, 129; tax problems, 3, 19-20, 38, 40, 42, 49, 62, 64, 69, 74, 76, 98-106, 111

Baltimore, Maryland: appeals procedure in, 107; blighted neighborhoods in, 43, 110; financial crisis of, 95; statutes, 140-141; summary, 130; tax-base equalization, 121; tax problems, 3, 19-20, 23, 26, 41-42, 53, 61-62, 76, 86-87, 98-106, 111; tax-base equalization in, 121; transitional neighborhoods in, 88
Baltimore City, Maryland, 90-92
Beneficiaries of tax reducltions, 17
Birmingham, Alabama, 21
Blacks, 51, 67-68; antagonism, 40; families of, 47, 72, 94; influx of, 59; low-income, 41, 60; middle-income, 72; real estate operators, 55; as tenants, 38, 40
Blighted neighborhoods, 5-7, 12, 22-34, 42, 61, 66-67, 70, 73, 89, 97, 102, 107,

111-115, 119; in Baltimore, 43, 110; and buildings, 79, 99; definition of, 125; in Portland, 38; upgrading of, 120
Borrowed funds, 84
Brooklyn area of Portland, 60, 63
Brown University, 80
Budget: assessor's, 104; funds, 8, 75; local, 92
Buena Vista East area of San Francisco, 81
Building and buildings: absentee owned, 61; age of, 26-29, 59, 105; blighted, 79, 99; codes, 110, 116; developers, 91; improvements, 83; inspection requirements, 53; permits, 69, 102; quality levels, 126; size of, 28
Burchell, Robert, cited, 13-14
Bureaucracy, delays of, 74, 111

California, 102; State Board of Equilization, 121
Capital: appreciation, 45, 82, 88; gains, 44, 53, 88; income; 83, 100; losses, 7; short-term, 45; supply of, 88; tax on, 99
Cash: positive return, 44; real value, 108; rent receipts, 69
Cash flow, 120; change in, 11; definition of, 126; near-zero, 11; negative, 12, 44, 48, 51, 54, 74, 120; positive, 11; reduced, 75; squeeze, 67; statements, 12-13; studies, 6
Census of Governments, cited, 19-21, 97-98
Center-city housing markets, 8, 119
Chicago, Illinois; appeals procedures in, 107; statues in, 141-142; summary, 131; tax problems in, 3, 13, 19-20, 23, 38-42, 53, 62, 68, 74, 76, 81, 86-88, 98-106, 110-111
Cigarette tax revenue, 121
City services, 69, 93, 121, 129
Closed-in neighborhood, 71
Code: building, 110, 116; enforcement, 51, 71; standards, 43, 49; violations, 81, 116
College Hill section of Providence, 80, 82
Commercial: investment, 71; property, 5, 90-93, 102-103, 107; rehabbers, 87
Communities, wealth of, 2
Competition: fiscal, 91; housing market, 23, 54-55; among investors, 49; public service, 8; suburban, 89; among suppliers, 17
Computers, use of, 102, 105, 121

199

About the Contributors

George E. Peterson received the B.A. from Amherst College; the B.A. and M.A. degrees from Balliol College, Oxford; the Ph.D. degree from Harvard University and was a Rhodes Scholar, 1963-65. He is on the senior research staff at The Urban Institute, Washington, D.C., and a member of the Board of Trustees at Amherst College. In addition to being a consultant to Arthur D. Little, Inc., he has served as consultant to the Educational and Cultural Secretariat of the Organization of American States; director of Educational Reform Planning and Budgeting, Government of Chile, and educational planning advisor for the Ford Foundation. He is the author of numerous articles and books on housing, income and taxation.

Arthur P. Solomon is associate professor at Massachusetts Institute of Technology and associate director of the M.I.T.-Harvard Joint Center for Urban Studies. Prior to joining the faculty at M.I.T. and receiving the Ph.D. from Harvard University, he was a staff member of President Johnson's Commission on Government Organization. He is the author of several articles and books on housing, property tax reform and human resource development. Among his most recent publications is *Housing the Urban Poor: A Critical Analysis of Federal Housing Policy*.

Hadi Madjid is project director and senior economist at Arthur D. Little, Inc., where his work focuses on the areas of housing and health. He is a trustee of Boston Biomedical Research Institute, on the Board of Directors of the Carroll Rehabilitation Center for the Visually Impaired and on the Board of Directors of the Beacon Hill Civic Association.

William C. Apgar, Jr. is a research analyst for the National Bureau of Economic Research (NBER) and consultant to Arthur D. Little, Inc. He is currently developing The NBER Urban Simulation Model to analyze housing market dynamics, and to investigate a variety of housing policy strategies relating to low income housing and the abandonment phenomenon under a HUD grant.

DA